$20.00 hardcover
$ 9.95 softcover

Alternatives to Traditional Family Living

The *Marriage & Family Review* series:

Alternatives to Traditional Family Living

Harriet Gross and Marvin B. Sussman
Editors

note: This is Volume 5, Number 2 of

Marriage & Family Review
Volume 5, Number 2

The Haworth Press
New York

The Haworth Press, Inc., 28 East 22 Street, New York, NY 10010

Library of Congress Cataloging in Publication Data
Main entry under title:

Alternatives to traditional family living.
    (Marriage & family review ; v. 5, no. 2)
    Includes bibliographies.
    1. Family—United States—Addresses, essays, lectures.
I. Gross, Harriet. II. Sussman, Marvin B. III. Series.
HQ536.A54   1982   306.8′5′0973   82-9250
ISBN 0-917724-59-3   AACR2
ISBN 0-917724-82-8 (pbk.)

Alternatives to Traditional Family Living

Marriage & Family Review
Volume 5, Number 2

Contents

INTRODUCTION

Political concerns of the eighties center on family life issues to an extent largely unthinkable as recently as ten years ago. Attention by conservatives to such issues as family structure, relations between the sexes, and women's reproductive rights, affirms the feminist contention that, indeed, "the personal is political." Yet beyond this inadvertent equivalence, conservatives share little common ground with feminists and other proponents of alternatives to traditional family living. In fact a large measure of the "new right" prescription for family well-being—the traditional nuclear ensemble of husband/breadwinner, wife/homemaker, complete with school age children—exists in opposition to alternatives spawned by the sixties and seventies. But theirs is a Luddite-like denial of societal changes, e.g., women's widely heralded increasing labor force participation and educational achievements, which call for new family forms.

In time the argument and often time heated debate on the family form best suited to our society's values and vital interests may prove to be more semantic than substantive. Some of the so-called new forms have always been in existence from the earliest period of our history. Their incidence and eruption as predominant forms along the life course differed over historic time. Events, situations, demographics, fertility, and mortality rates effected these individual and family transitions. In one historic era, in a given locale, single parent or multigenerational family forms may have been predominant over other forms. In another time period and under particular conditions the nuclear family of procreation in neolocal residence may have been a dominant form. Recent economic events and social conditions have spawned a "dual work" family, both parents in gainful employment, with obvious consequences for parenting and internal relationships.

Far from representing efforts to destroy "The Family" many alternatives are attempts to shore up familistic values under changing social circumstances. The articles in this volume review issues and problems associated with these attempts. Three articles deal with family forms on the increase in the seventies: single parent, voluntary childless and commuter families. One article on the kibbutz examines changes in family structure and women's position in that firmament for studying the effects of social change. The final article examines the state of family foster care and the directions this form of family life is taking.

Pat Gongla's discussion of female-headed, single parent families shows how concept clarification and refinement improves our understanding of this major alternative family form. Her analysis points to three problems that have plagued the study of this family type: the focus on the individual rather than on the family; the lack of examination of the family's relationship to its social environment; and the assumption of an absent father.

Voluntary childlessness is the subject of the next article by Sharon Houseknecht. She examines data indicating trends in the rate of development of this family type and considers the significance of this life-style for gender equality in marital relationships and society in general. Her finding that the voluntary childless, who by comparison with parenting couples have more egalitarian domestic divisions of labor, points up the irony of an alternative family form which seems to benefit just those spouses, who free of parenting responsibilities, have relatively fewer obligations.

Gerstel and Gross' review of commuter couples reveals that this marital form, like its traditional counterpart and other families that require separated living, represents a system of trade-offs, which balances the costs and benefits characteristic of all complex relationships. Though destined to remain in response to working women's increasing professionalization a life-style option for a considerable number, living apart is apparently an emotionally costly alternative family form.

The next article about the kibbutz updates our understanding of the evolution of family through the stages of kibbutz history and the implications this evolution has for the status of women. Hertz's analysis transcends a limiting focus on the internal structure and function of the kibbutz family form. Her discussion informs on the family's relation to the larger community and the social construction vs. biological determination of sex roles.

While the focus of the seventies accustomed us to thinking about alternative life-styles in terms of sexual options and structural variations in family forms among real and fictive kinsmen, the last article about foster families draws our attention to an older family form that represents an alternative to traditional family living. Though foster families typically uphold parenting norms necessitating heterosexuality and duality, Eastman shows that this non-normative parenting arrangement has also had to contend with changing circumstances related to women's increasing labor force participation and the increase in single adult households. She introduces her review of recruitment, selection, legal issues and factors associated with successful placements, with a history of the changes characterizing foster families since the inception of this family form in the 19th century.

Throughout these reviews runs an affirmation of the viability of family in its many alternative variations. The political right's concern for "The Family's" demise, like Twain's death, is "greatly exaggerated." But, of course, the family's death is not what they fear, so much as the liberating potential of these alternatives.

The Editors

SINGLE PARENT FAMILIES:
A LOOK AT FAMILIES OF MOTHERS
AND CHILDREN

Patricia A. Gongla, PhD

The single parent family consisting of a mother and her children has become a significant family form in recent times. Compared with all families in the United States, the percentage that are maintained by women without a husband has increased from 10 percent in 1960 to about 15 percent in 1979. In contrast, the percentage of husband-wife families has declined from 87 percent to 83 percent, and the percentage of families maintained by men (without a wife present) has remained relatively constant at a low percentage, about 3 percent (U.S. Bureau of the Census, 1979: Table 62; 1980).

Much of this increase in the number of mother-child families results from increases in divorce and separation (Ross and Sawhill, 1975:13), and single mothers now are much more likely to form their own households rather than move in with relatives (Bianchi and Farley, 1979; Cutright, 1974; Smith, 1980; Sweet, 1972). Recently, there has also been an increase in never-married motherhood, although the number of these single parent families is still relatively small. In 1979, about 1.5 million children lived with never-married mothers as compared with 7.2 million children living with their divorced or separated mothers (U.S. Bureau of the Census, 1980: Table H).

As the number of single parent families has increased, so has the public concern about them. This public interest, however, has manifested itself as a concern for a growing "social problem." Instead of viewing the single parent family as simply an alternative family form, the public has usually viewed it as a deviant family, not living up to the ideal and norm of a two-parent family. The social stigma of marital separation and divorce or "illegitimate birth" hangs over many of the families. In addition,

Dr. Gongla is a Research Sociologist at Veterans Administration Medical Center, Brentwood, Los Angeles, CA.

the families are "headed" by women, and women, by tradition, are not supposed to be such authority figures. A further issue is that a considerable number of one-parent families are Black (e.g., in 1979, while only 15 percent of all children under 18 were Black, 37 percent of all children living in one-parent households with their mothers were Black [U.S. Bureau of the Census, 1980:Table H]). These families face additional problems from racial discrimination.

The public view of single parent families as deviant has also been adopted by many researchers who assume the two-parent family to be the norm and who expect problems to develop in one-parent households. This perspective has prevented the growth of comprehensive knowledge about single parent families. "The unfortunate assumption that there is a one-to-one relationship between this type of family structure and all kinds of social and psychological pathology has resulted in almost total ignorance about these families—the majority—who somehow have circumvented this 'inevitable pathology'" (Billingsley and Giovannoni, 1971:368). With few exceptions, it is not until recently that researchers have begun to avoid the deviance perspective and to study single parent families as an alternative family form.

Along with the deviance perspective, other problems developed in the research on one-parent families, hindering the growth of knowledge. The objective of this article will be to examine three of the major problems in past research: (1) the focus on the individual rather than the family: (2) the lack of examination of the family's relationship to its social environment; and (3) the assumption of an absent father. After discussing each problem, recent research that attempts to avoid or to correct the problem will be examined. The goal is to show that this recent re-focusing of the literature is beginning to provide insight into the functioning of single parent families.

Focus on the Individual Versus the Family

Much of the research purportedly dealing with single parent families does not, in fact, study the family but rather examines individuals who are living in single parent families. Instead of studying the family as the dependent variable, family structure is used as the independent variable.

Although occasionally focusing on mothers (e.g., Phelps, 1969, Pipher, 1977), a typical study here would be a "father absence" study, where children are divided into two groups: those from father present (dual-parent) families and those from father absent (single parent) families.

Differences in the individual's characteristics are sought between the two groups, with the differences attributed to the presence or absence of the father. Common dependent variables include: cognitive development or academic achievement (e.g., The Consortium, 1980; Lessing, Zagorin and Nelson, 1970; Santrock, 1972), sex development (e.g., Badaines, 1976; Biller and Bahm, 1971; Nelsen and Vangen, 1971) and various social or psychological problems such as delinquency or emotional disturbance (e.g., Kalter, 1977; Lester and Beck, 1976; Zold, 1975).

This widespread form of research has had two major consequences that have limited our understanding of single parent families: the concentration on homogeneity and (as mentioned) the focus on the individual.

Homogeneity

In this literature, the distinguishing feature of the family is whether it has experienced some event, such as death or divorce, which causes the father not to live with the family. All families meeting the criterion are classified in the same manner—as father absent (single parent) families. Being classified in the same way, the families are viewed as a homogeneous group and as distinguishable from other family types.

While not denying that these families may share certain characteristics, assumptions about single parent families as a simple structural type have diverted interest from exploring both the complexity that exists within the family and the diversity existing among families. It has also hindered the search for commonalities between one-parent and two-parent family systems.

Emphasis on the Individual

The second issue with this type of research is its focus on the individual as distinct from the family. It is true that researchers point to the family structure—the father's presence or absence—as a prime determinant of the individual's (child's) development. But this is very different from considering the person as a full-fledged family member, filling certain roles, contributing to family decision-making, participating in the family's conflicts, and so on. Thus we do not gain knowledge of family processes from the research. Indeed, it is questionable whether we even gain knowledge of the individual's development. The simple variable of father absence/presence may obscure the explanation of certain patterns of individual development, since father absence is correlated with other variables, like socioeconomic factors, which affect development (Herzog and Sudia, 1970).

Re-focusing

As researchers continued to re-conceptualize, more independent and control variables were added to father absence to gain explanatory power. Most variables were either structural or demographic, such as race (Hartnagel, 1970; Hunt and Hunt, 1975), number and sex of siblings (Biller, 1968; Wohlford, Santrock, Berger and Liberman, 1971), and age at onset of father absence (Biller and Bahm, 1971; Santrock, 1977).

More importantly, the recognition slowly grew that a mother lived in the "father absent" family and her attitudes and behaviors would affect the child's development (Biller, 1970; 1971; Hetherington, 1972; Hetherington and Deur, 1971; Hoffman, 1971; McCord, McCord and Thurber, 1962; Phelps. 1969).

Other investigators began focusing on the family environment in trying to explain the individual's behavior. Here we see the debate over whether the single parent home, if it is warm, accepting and non-conflict-ridden, is a better environment for children than a two-parent home that is filled with hostility, rejection, and conflict. Although some studies find marital separation to produce generally negative effects (e.g., Landis, 1960; Hetherington, 1973), the weight of the evidence suggests that a warm family environment and positive parent-child relationships are more important than structure (one-parent vs. two-parent) in producing positive outcomes for the child (e.g., Berg and Kelly, 1979; Burchinal, 1964; Herzog and Sudia, 1970; Lamb, 1977; Magreb, 1978; Nye, 1957; Raschke and Raschke, 1979).

Although all of these studies are still concerned with the individual's development, they are important for three reasons. First they show that single parent families are not a homogeneous group, even though the families may have some common features. Structural, psychological and interactional differences among these families have varying impacts on the individual family members. Second, the research points out that some variables, such as family conflict, may supercede structure in dominance of effects on individuals. Thus, some single parent families are more similar to some two-parent families then they are to other single parent families. Third, these studies, particularly those dealing with family conflict and mother-child relationships, suggest the need for understanding more about family functioning.

This third point is most important; we approach the idea of studying the family system instead of concentrating on the individual family members. The perspective of most research until recently appeared to be: when a marriage dissolves, the family dissolves; if a marriage never starts, a family never starts. But, as Sprey (1979:155) says: "Divorce (or death) ends a marriage but not a family." The family changes, but it remains a family. If we are to learn anything about this family form, we must focus on it as a functioning system and examine it in its own right (Burgess, 1970). If "Contemporary families . . . are small systems characterized by a high degree of interdependence, reciprocity, and common identity" (Sprey, 1979:153), what do we know about interdependence, reciprocity and common identity in one-parent families? If families develop a shared mode for interpreting or construing the environment (McCubbin and Boss, 1980), what do we know about how the family reconstrues the environment after divorce or father's death? What do we know about conflict management in the family or the creation of emotional solidarity or the definition and fulfillment of roles? What do we know about this family we call "single-parent?"

We can start with a conceptual work by Glasser and Navarre (1974) who proposed some structural characteristics of the one-parent family. We can look at the characteristics individually, and see if research evidence supports the conceptualization.

The first structural characteristic: since the responsibility for most family tasks belongs to the parents, and normally this is a full-time job for two adults, tasks likely to be unfilled are those of the "traditionally female specialization." Research evidence supports this proposition (Brandwein, Brown and Fox, 1974; Hunt and Hunt, 1977; Loge, 1977; Weiss, 1975). For example, Rasmussen (1975) reported that both male and female single parents used more instrumental than expressive behaviors, and no statistically significant difference was found between men and women in the proportion of instrumental to expressive behaviors. However, there is some questioning of the initial assumption of Glasser and Navarre's proposition, that is, that the responsibility for most family tasks belongs to the parents. Because there are so many tasks, yet only one parent, the responsibility for tasks normally performed by parents in an intact family may begin to be shared with the children in a one-parent household, particularly if the children are adolescents (Weiss, 1979).

Second, Glasser and Navarre stated that the child is exposed to only one power figure and may thus perceive authority as personal rather than consensual and come to identify power with a single sex. However, the research evidence does not support this idea. Rather, the evidence indicates that, at least in divorce situations, there may be power struggles and a power redistribution after the father leaves, with mothers often *not* gaining in power (Hunt and Hunt, 1977; Wallerstein and Kelly, 1980:111-117). With the mother having no adult ally to help assert authority, a blurring of distinctions between level of adult and level of child may occur, leading to more negotiation of rules and standards (Weiss, 1975) and new rights and authority being granted to children (Weiss, 1979). In addition, women may be at a disadvantage in trying to assert authority within the family since social norms and institutions in general inhibit women from exercising such power (Brandwein, Brown and Fox, 1974; Weiss, 1979).

The last of Glasser and Navarre's propositions to be considered here is that the child cannot provide an appropriate outlet for the single parent's negative emotions; a child's love is demanding rather than supporting. Limited research provides qualified support here. For example, Weiss (1975:173) observes: "The relationships of single-parent mothers and their children, although they may be gratifying in their own way, fail to provide certain relational elements and are almost burdensome and restrictive . . ." But when children are adolescents, they may indeed be at least as supportive as they are demanding, becoming companions for the parent (Weiss, 1979:11). Also, positive adjustment to the single-parenting role may take considerable time and may be associated with finding new roles outside the family unit and acquiring an identity as a single person as well as a single parent (Loge, 1977).

Problems may develop if the parent, because of her own troubles, cannot recognize that the child is not an appropriate outlet for all negative emotions. Wallerstein and Kelly (1980:118) note the extreme case: ". . . at its most insidious was the situation of divorce where the custodial parent lost clarity of her own ego boundaries and included the child or children within the orbit of her unhappiness and disorganization. Acute depression in the parent was difficult for the children . . ."

Compared with mothers in two-parent families, some research indicates that single mothers may have more negative patterns of parenting. Single mothers may be more autocratic and rigid about structuring activities (St. Pierre, 1980) and about allowing children to express aggression, to learn about sex, or to be exposed to adult influences outside the home (Phelps, 1969). Less autonomy may be allowed (Longabaugh, 1973; Phelps, 1969), and less affection expressed, especially to sons (M. L. Hoffman, 1971). Fewer demands for mature behavior may be made (Hetherington, Cox and Cox, 1979) particularly if the family moves in with relatives (Gongla, 1974). In turn, children may be more aggressive in single parent homes and comply less frequently with the mother's demands (Hetherington, Cox and Cox, 1977).

Yet this negative picture may not be comprehensive reflection of the single parent household. First, the negative effects are most apparent in the period following marital disruption, with parent-child interaction becoming smoother (Wallerstein and Kelly, 1980:159) and more similar to that of intact families as time goes on (Hetherington, Cox and Cox, 1979). Furthermore, it may indeed be that, with no relief from another parent, the single mother may overreact with a strict punishment or rejection in the face of children's opposition. But the mother also may overlook many things, lacking the energy to discipline and not wanting to threaten the sense of partnership with the children that the parent is coming to rely upon (Weiss, 1979). Finally, if restrictive and more punishment-oriented childrearing practices do occur, they may be related to a lack of social support or satisfaction with the support (Colletta, 1979a) or to low income levels (Goode, 1956; Colletta, 1979b).

Not surprisingly, in the one parent home as in the two parent family, both parenting and children's behaviors will vary considerably by the age and number of children present (Wallerstein and Kelly, 1980: 166; Weiss, 1979).

Summary

Although studies on changes in individual family members can indeed be useful, "what is sorely needed from here on in is a shifting of our research focus from the conduct of individual spouses and children toward families as systems" (Sprey, 1979:156). The available research is just beginning to show a few outlines of how single parent families function. The major points that have been tentatively supported are: (1) if the family is warm and not conflict-ridden, a child can develop normally in a single parent home; (2) with so many tasks to be performed and only one parent available on an everyday basis, children gain in responsibility and power, thus shifting the authority structure of the family from its pre-single-parent days; (3) disruption, restrictiveness by the mother and aggression by the children may be part of the initial reaction to the changed family status, but in most cases, they diminish over time if supports are present; (4) interdependence of family members grows.

Family in a Social Vacuum

If much of the literature on single parent families viewed the individual as almost unrelated to the family, so has the literature often failed to link the family (or individual) with the larger social environment. It has often seemed that kin, friends, community groups, and institutions did not exist for the one parent family. Key variables such as support, reciprocity, alliance, integration, and normative expectations have been ill-examined. Most of the research gave little or no consideration to how the individual or the family interacted with and were affected by the environment outside the immediate family unit. We are left with a picture of the single parent family as divorced from the larger world—existing in a social vacuum.

Re-focusing

In considering the relationship of single parent families to the larger social environment, we can take both macro and micro perspectives. By "macro" is meant the large-scale social institutions such as economics, politics, education, and religion. In the micro perspective we consider "smaller" groups, that are encountered in face-to-face interaction or to which there is an emotional tie, such as friends, relatives, neighbors and co-workers.

Macro Environment. The position of single parent families vis-à-vis large-scale social institutions seems to have been governed by two factors. First is the idea that one-parent families are deviant, even pathological (Schorr and Moen, 1979:15). The second factor is the heading of these single parent families by women. This also is deviance, since women traditionally are not supposed to head families. Further, the social status granted women in general is lower than men's. The combination of these two factors has contributed to a lack of accommodation and recognition by social institutions to single parent mothers and children. We do know that generally there is a lack of child care options, occupational opportunities, flexible business and social service provision, social prestige, and power (Brandwein, Brown and Fox, 1974; Ross and Sawhill, 1975; Schorr and Moen, 1979). However, the research has not, for the most part, detailed the nature, extent, and effects of this lack of accommodation or discrimination upon single parent families (Brandwein, Brown and Fox, 1974).

One partial exception is economics. Here there is evidence that the economic status of female-headed single parent families is relatively low (Ross and Sawhill, 1975). Throughout the 1960s, for example, the income of families headed by men remained more than double that of female-headed families. In 1973, of all the female-headed families with children, 44 percent lived in poverty (S. Hoffman, 1977). Wattenberg and Reinhardt (1979:460) noted that: "Female-headed families now represent the single largest subgroup of the population that lives below the poverty level."

By 1970, about three-fifths of female-headed families with children were on welfare rolls (Stein, 1970). A 1974 survey of a representative sample of all Pennsylvania households showed that 71 percent of the female-headed households were either using or were qualified for cash or social service assistance (Sibbison, 1974). Although it has been suggested that the availability of welfare funds may increase the length of time that a woman remains a family head as she delays remarriage (Bahr, 1979), even with welfare funds, female heads are in a relatively poorer economic position vis-à-vis married women (Bradbury et al., 1979:535). Although widowed women with children have slightly higher income than the divorced or separated, they too remain in a fairly poor economic position (Mallan, 1975).

Women suffer loss of income relative to family needs *after* becoming single parents (Kriesberg, 1970:177). Hoffman (1977) examined data from a longitudinal study of 2400 men and women married in 1968. By 1974, those couples who remained married experienced a 20.8 percent increase in income relative to needs. Divorced or separated men had a 16.5 percent increase, but for divorced or separated women, income relative to needs decreased 6.7 percent. Bradbury and colleagues (1979) estimated that women experience a 40 percent decrease in income when they move from a husband-wife family to heading a household. As with Hoffman's findings, this reduction occurred even though more female heads than married women were employed, worked more hours, and had more personal income from wages and non-public assistance sources. The lowered economic status has been related to factors such as low and irregular levels of public assistance and of child support payments, lower salaries and fewer employment opportunities than are available to men, and fewer adult earners to support the family (Espenshade, 1979; Bane, 1976).

The lowered economic status has major impacts on these mother-headed families. Families are often forced to reduce consumption and to move to poorer neighborhoods. This leads to confrontation with the problems of reduced personal safety, higher delinquency rates and poorer schools (Brandwein, Brown and Fox, 1974). More single parent mothers than married mothers are employed and must contend with problems of finding child-care services. Low economic status undoubtedly has effects on child development, although this factor is rarely controlled for adequately (Herzog and Sudia, 1970). Low income, as well as the unstable or demeaning sources of income that many single mothers must rely upon, may be related to a low sense of personal fate control and ability to plan for the family's future (Bould, 1977).

Given the major effects economics can have on family functioning, economic status should always be considered when dealing with single parent families. Similarly, we should begin to assess how the single parent family relates to other major social institutions.

Micro Environment. Social relationships with kin, friends, and other informal contacts have been studied primarily from the single parent's point of view rather than from the child's or the family unit's view. Although limited information is available about the nature of these relationships, we are increasingly aware of the importance of social ties.

Examining first the relationships with kin: it does seem that single parents maintain or increase their contact and affectional ties with blood relatives after marital separation or divorce, and decrease ties with in-laws (Anspach, 1976; Gongla, 1977; Hiltz, 1978; Spicer and Hampe, 1975; Stack, 1974). Children's patterns of contact with kin tend to resemble their mother's patterns (Anspach, 1976). However, children's relationships with the father's kin group may depend upon ties being maintained with the father himself, since he is the access route to his own blood relatives (Anspach, 1976; Gongla, 1977; O'Brien and Garland, 1977).

Relatives generally feel a commitment to help, and they provide a sense of security apart from actual help they give. However, they may not understand or approve of the single parent's situation and offer criticism and unwanted advice (Weiss, 1979). Therefore, maintaining some distance and independence from relatives seems valuable. This is particularly apparent if we look at the family that goes to live with the mother's relatives, usually her parents. In most cases this arrangement leads to tension and to strong dissatisfaction with the home environment among divorced mothers (Colletta, 1979a). Women who return to their families are likely to decline in status, with their parents reasserting their parenting roles (Weiss, 1975). Difficulties in maintaining role boundaries may arise, with children having problems determining where authority lies (Dell and Appelbaum, 1977). Compared with children living only with their mothers, children in families living with relatives are less likely to increase their household responsibilities or to give emotional support to the mother (Gongla, 1974).

Regarding the mother's relationships with friends, there is some evidence that a network of married friends may be lost over time for the divorced and widowed. For the previously married, especially for divorcees, a sense of becoming marginal to the "married" community—one's former community—will probably develop (Kitson et al., 1980). For those not previously married, friendships with single, non-time-constrained friends without children will likely fade (Weiss, 1975; 1979). A degree of social isolation may ensue (Hetherington, Cox and Cox, 1979). However, ties with a few close friends from "before," especially females, are likely to be maintained (Gongla, 1977). And, although single parents may have lower levels of community participation than do heads of two-parent families (Smith, 1980), as time goes on a new network of friends is often formed (Goode, 1956; Hunt and Hunt, 1977). These friends are expected to understand the single parent's situation but not to intrude on her valued autonomy (Greenberg, 1979; Weiss, 1979). Having friends, particularly a network of close female friends, reduces loneliness and helps eliminate problems with leisure time (Greenberg, 1979). These friends may even provide more support for the single parents than do relatives (Loge, 1977). Friendships, however, require reciprocity: if help is accepted, help must be offered in return. If the single parent is not in the position of being able to offer help, it becomes difficult to maintain the relationship.

Examining the ties between single parents and their support networks is necessary for understanding how the family functions. As Weiss (1979:167) says:

> Single adults, more than the married, need ties outside their homes, for they are without that fellow adult within the household who can provide the married with assistance and companionship. But the single parent's need for ties outside the home is greater even than that of other single adults because the single parent, as head of a family, is more likely to need the help of others.

The crucial nature of this support from outside the home is also suggested by research in epidemiology. This research indicates that formerly married people are likely to have poorer physical health than do married people (Bloom, Asher and White, 1978; Rico-Velasco and Mynko,

1973). Results from studies on psychological disturbances are similar: the formerly-married fare less well than the married (Bachrach, 1975; Berkman, 1969; Briscoe and Smith, 1974; Fox, 1980; Parker and Kleiner, 1966; Renne, 1971). Although the distinction between parents and non-parents in the different martial statuses is not usually made, the little evidence available agrees in showing that married parents are healthier than non-married parents (Berkman, 1969; Parker and Kleiner, 1966).

Although findings are more tentative than conclusive, the research suggests that support from social networks is a major factor in reducing the occurrence of illness and death (Berkman and Syme, 1979; Cassel, 1976; Cobb, 1976; Mueller, 1980; Turner, 1980). Married people may be gaining the support from their spouses so that marriage "protects" them from illnesses (Bloom, Asher and White, 1978; Kessler, 1979; Pearlin and Johnson, 1977). For single parents, support must come from outside the home, since children are not generally asked for help by parents who are distressed (Chiriboga, 1979). Given their generally higher illness rates, however, it may be that single parents do not receive adequate support from their social networks to meet their needs. We can hypothesize: if physical or mental health problems occur, the single parent is in need of even more support, but is probably less likely to receive it, particularly from friends, if the parent's ability to reciprocate has been impaired by the illness.

The research on children's social networks is very limited. Wallerstein and Kelly (1980) did note that, except for adolescent boys, children's relationships with their peers seemed to depend upon their relationship with the custodial parent and the quality of homelife.

> Children did not use their friends to escape from an unhappy, conflict-ridden household. Instead, they were free to make use of friends when the conflicted home was relatively quiet and when the relationships within the family were good and supportive of their efforts. . . . (Then) it appears that friends were helpful and expanded and enriched the quality of the child's life, but as a source of support when the home situation was trying they were of limited help to most of these youngsters (Wallerstein and Kelly, 1980:221).

Perhaps because they do not use a clinical sample as Wallerstein and Kelly had, Kurdek and Siesky (1980) see peer groups as being more supportive for children. Three-fourths of their sample of children felt that their parents' divorce did not matter to their friends. Because divorce has become common, "Children now have a peer support system available to them which may buffer negative effects arising from the child's dealing with the immediate and long-term distress of the parent's separation" (Kurdek and Siesky, 1980:375).

Research is certainly needed if we are to understand how children from single parent families adapt to and utilize their social networks and what the consequences of these relationships are both for the child and for the family.

Summary

Given our past lack of emphasis on the single parent family's relationship with the larger social environment, we have limited knowledge. Single parent families headed by women are generally economically poorer than married dual parent families; single mothers probably have higher rates of illness which may be related to lack of social support; relationships with blood kin are usually maintained but those with in-laws (particularly after divorce) are diminished; networks of friends may change; and the need for support from outside the family may increase.

The Absent Father

Until recently, most studies on single parent families failed to consider how the father continued to relate to the family. Rather, investigators considered the father to be absent, to have no effect on the family except by his absence. Indeed, single parent families were identified by the assumption of an absent father—absence being assumed whenever marital separation, divorce, death, or unwed pregnancy occurred. When these families were compared with "intact," two-parent families, whatever differences occurred were attributed primarily to the absence of the father. With the exception of an occasional conceptual work (e.g., Rosenfeld and Rosenstein, 1973), whether the father was indeed actually absent was rarely considered.

Re-focusing

Along with the growing awareness of fatherhood in general, attention is being directed toward the father in these single parent families. As with other topics, most of the work done thus far is concentrated on families experiencing marital separation and divorce; awareness is growing that the parental status remains after the marital status dissolves. The unmarried fathers of children have received less attention with research concentrated on Black families often in the context of describing kinship patterns or the Black male's subculture (Earls and Siegel, 1980; Furstenberg and Talvitie, 1980; Grow, 1979; Liebow, 1967; Presser, 1978; Stack, 1974; Vincent, 1961). Here, continuing bonds between father and child and the two parents are often maintained to some degree. Considering families where the death of the father has occurred, research is needed not only on how the memory of the father is evoked during family interaction, but also on the psychological presence of the father and how it affects family behaviors.

Focusing on families after marital separation and divorce, the concept of "boundary" is useful: how and to what extent is the father involved in role performance and considered to be inside or outside the family? For a time after separation, the answer to this question would be ambiguous as the family attempts to reorganize. This period is likely to be stressful, since "Stress continues in any family until membership can be clarified and the system reorganized regarding (a) who performs what roles and tasks, and (b) how family members perceive the absent member" (Boss, 1980:449).

Norms and role dimensions for the father after divorce have not been a part of our culture. Yet, recent research, albeit scanty, offers some suggestions of what may be emerging norms. The suggestions apply to the three possible roles for the father: (1) the parental role—the direct father-child relationship; (2) the co-parental role—the relationship between mother and father based on their mutual concern for the child; and (3) the non-parental role—the relationship between ex-spouses *not* concerned with child-related issues.

First, regarding the parental role: there seems to be general agreement that the father has a direct responsibility for the child and should maintain regular contact with him or her (Weiss, 1979). In Wallerstein and Kelly's study (1980:125), for example, only one-fifth of the mothers saw no value in the father's continued visits with children, and Goldsmith (1979) found that 91 percent of the parents in her study felt it important for the father to stay involved with the child. Although still unusual, the growing number of joint custody decisions also indicates the increasing support for the father's continued involvement with his children (Abarbanel, 1979; Ahrons, 1978; 1980).

Second, with regard to the co-parental role: the emerging norm may be that parents, after separation, should maintain involvement with each other as parents and should share information about their children. For example, Goldsmith (1979) found that 84 percent of her sample of parents maintained a relationship as parents after divorce. Goetting (1980) reported that, after remarriage, respondents agreed that even the new spouse of a custodial parent should inform the non-custodial parent of important information (e.g., emergencies) about the child.

Third, concerning the non-parental role: it is difficult to suggest emerging norms here. The amount of research is small and the "role" appears ambiguous. It may be that most ex-spouses avoid discussing any "intense" issues, restricting conversation to "safe" topics, such as family or friends (Ahrons, 1978; Goldsmith, 1979). A tone of distant friendliness and routinization may be sought (Weiss, 1979).

Aside from the emergence of norms, research indicates that feelings between ex-spouses tend to be ambivalent (Goldsmith, 1979; Weiss, 1979). Feelings of attachment may persist long after the separation (Brown et al., 1980; Weiss, 1975; 1976), although Goldsmith (1979) found only a third of her sample to maintain such feelings of attachment.

Partially because of these ambivalent feelings, visits between father and child create emotional stress and disruption for the mother. In addition, visits are often difficult to schedule, and children often exhibit troublesome behavior afterward (Wallerstein and Kelly, 1980; Weiss, 1979).

Looking at the effects of father-child relationships on the child, five years after marital separation, Wallerstein and Kelly (1980:219) found that "good father-child relationships appeared linked to high self-esteem and the absence of depression in children of both sexes and at all ages." Although about 70 percent of father-child relationships became emotionally limited over time, the continuation of some contact was beneficial except in cases of the father's psychological disturbance. Children themselves may perceive divorce as less traumatic if they are allowed free, unrestricted access to the non-custodial parent (Rosen, 1979).

Other research has emphasized the strong effects that the father's interaction with the family has on children's behavior. "When support and agreement occurred between divorced couples, the disruption in family functioning appeared to be less extreme, and the restabilizing of family functioning occurred earlier, by the end of the first year" (Hetherington, Cox and Cox, 1977:32). Similarly, Jacobson (1978) found that the lower the level of hostility between the parents during separation, the better the adjustment of the child.

Summary

There is a growing awareness among researchers that fathers may continue to play an important role in their families after divorce, separation, or out-of-marriage birth. Evidence suggests that most parents feel the father has a responsibility to his children and should maintain contact with them and with their mother concerning important child-related matters. Maintaining such contact in many cases seems to have beneficial consequences for the children and the family. In families where the father's death has occurred, his psychological presence may have continued impact, and ambiguity of boundaries within the family may result. It is painfully obvious that we have a great deal more to learn about how the father is integrated with the family and the consequences of his integration for all members.

Conclusions

The intent of this article has been to point out some of the major problems with past literature on single parent families and to show the needed re-direction of more recent research. Leaving the deviance and pathology perspective behind, we must concentrate on the single parent family *as a family,* examining its internal organization and reorganization over time. Hence, we must remember that the initial reactions of the family to the death, divorce, or unwed pregnancy are indicative of a stressed period when family boundaries and role expectations are being re-negotiated; reorganization proceeds over time. We must study the family as it relates to the larger social environment, both to large-scale social institutions and to smaller social networks like kin and friends. We must recognize that the father is still a member of the family by virtue of his parenthood status; his physical and psychological presence must be examined.

Because our knowledge about single parent families is limited, it is difficult to recommend any specific social policies that would benefit the family's functioning, apart from providing needed economic support, child care services, and long-term educational and vocational up-grading for single mothers (Brown et al., 1976). But these goals are far from simple, as witness, for example, the debate over provision of child care (Woolsey, 1977), or the complexity of issues surrounding an income maintenance policy (Shorr and Moen, 1979). In Ross and Sawhill's (1975) view, the goal of any public policy should be neutrality with respect to family organization, "not attempting to promote one family living pattern over another . . ." (Ross and Sawhill, 1975:178). This would allow more options and flexibility for families as they move from one form to another. A policy of neutrality would also allow a family form like joint custody after divorce to be tried, since initial indications are that this arrangement can work well under certain conditions (Abarbanel, 1979; Ahrons, 1980). In addition, given our limited knowledge, a suggestion by Wallerstein and Kelly (1979:474) seems apropos: "the time has come to introduce pilot programs rather than broad changes in social and family policy." They suggest the need for prevention and early intervention services such as mediation services, educational programs to inform adults of the children's needs, and consultation services to schools and day-care centers.

In terms of improving research, the re-direction of perspectives, noted throughout the article, should be maintained. In addition, we should be aware constantly of the complexity of our subject. For example, the age of the child at separation must be considered since the process of divorce, death, or of living in a one parent family affects children differently depending on the particular developmental task they are engaged in (Magreb, 1978; Wallerstein and Kelly, 1975; 1976; 1980). Consideration of the circumstances leading to single parenthood is important. Beyond distinguishing between divorce and death, the type of husband-wife interaction and parent-child interaction that occurred while the marriage was intact needs to be studied in relation to how the child and family develops afterward (Lamb, 1977). Sibling interaction and the process of incorporating new male adults into the family need more attention. Linking the family to the larger environment, social class and subcultural differences among families should be examined.

In summary, when we study the single parent family, we should, as Herzog and Sudia say (1968:181):

> give clearer recognition to the one-parent family as a family form in its own right. . . . We need to take account of its strengths as well as its weaknesses; of the characteristics it shares with two-parent families as well as its differences; of ways in which it copes with its undeniable difficulties; and of ways in which the community supports or undermines its coping capacity.

We must deal with the single parent family as a viable family system and study how it came to be, how it functions, and how it relates to the larger community.

REFERENCES

Abarbanel, Alice. "Shared parenting after separation and divorce: A study of joint custody." *American Journal of Orthopsychiatry* 49:320-329, 1979.

Ahrons, Constance R. *The co-parental divorce: Preliminary research findings and policy implications.* Paper presented at the meeting of the National Council on Family Relations, Philadelphia, 1978.

Ahrons, Constance R. "Joint custody arrangements in the postdivorce family." *Journal of Divorce* 3:189-205, 1980.

Anspach, Donald F. "Kinship and divorce." *Journal of Marriage and the Family* 38:323-330, 1976.

Bachrach, L. L. Marital status and mental disorder: An analytical review. (DHEW Publication No. ADM 75-217). Washington, D.C.: U.S. Government Printing Office, 1975.

Badaines, Joel. "Identification, imitation, and sex-role preference in father-present and father-absent Black and Chicano boys." *The Journal of Psychology* 92:15-24, 1976.

Bahr, Stephen J. "The effects of welfare on marital stability and remarriage." *Journal of Marriage and the Family* 41(3):553-560, 1979.

Bane, Mary Jo. "Marital disruption and the lives of children." *Journal of Social Issues* 32:103-117, 1976.

Baptiste, D. A. A comparative study of mothers' personality characteristics and child-rearing attitudes in husband-present and husband-absent families. *Dissertation Abstracts International,* 37, 6263-A—6264-A, 1976.

Barclay, A. and D. R. Cusumano. "Father absence, cross-sex identity, and field-dependent behavior in male adolescents." *Child Development* 38:243-250, 1967.

Berg, B. and R. Kelly. "The measured self-esteem of children from broken rejected and accepted families." *Journal of Divorce* 2:363-369, 1979.

Berkman, Lisa F. and S. Leonard Syme. "Social networks, host resistance, and mortality: A nine–year follow–up study of Alameda County residents." *American Journal of Epidemiology* 109:186-204, 1979.

Berkman, P. L. "Spouseless motherhood, psychological stress, and physical morbidity." *Journal of Health and Social Behavior,* 10:323-334, 1969.

Bianchi, Suzanne M. and Farley Reynolds. "Racial differences in family living arrangements and economic well being: An analysis of recent trends." *Journal of Marriage and the Family* 41(3):537-551, 1979.

Biller, Henry B. and Farley Reynolds. "A note on father absence and masculine development in lower-class Negro and white boys." *Child Development* 39:1003-1006, 1968.

Biller, Henry B. and Farley Reynolds. "Father absence and the personality development of the male child." *Developmental Psychology* 2:181-201, 1970.

Biller, Henry B. and Farley Reynolds. "The mother-child relationship and the father-absent boy's personality development." *Merrill-Palmer Quarterly* 17:227-241, 1971.

Biller, Henry B. and Robert M. Bahm. "Father absence, perceived maternal behavior, and masculinity of self-concept among junior high school boys." *Developmental Psychology* 4:178-81, 1971.

Billingsley, A. and J. M. Giovannoni. Family, one parent. In R. Morris (Ed.), *Encyclopedia of Social Work,* vol. 1. New York: National Association of Social Workers, 1971.

Blanchard, Robert W. and Henry B. Biller. "Father availability and academic performance among third-grade boys." *Developmental Psychology* 4:301-305, 1971.

Bloom, Bernard L., Shirley J. Asher and Stephen W. White. "Marital disruption as a stressor: A review and analysis." *Psychological Bulletin* 85(4):867-894, 1978.

Boss, Pauline G. "Normative family stress: Family boundary changes across the life-span." *Family Relations* 29:445-450, 1980.

Bould, Sally. "Female-headed families: Personal fate control and the provider role. *Journal of Marriage and the Family* 39:339-349, 1977.

Bradbury, Katharine, Sheldon Danziger, Eugene Smolensky and Paul Smolensky. "Public assistance, female headship, and economic well-being." *Journal of Marriage and the Family* 41(3):519-535, 1979.

Brandwein, Ruth A., Carole A. Brown and Elizabeth Maury Fox. "Women and children last: The social situation of divorced mothers and their families." *Journal of Marriage and the Family* 36:498-514, 1974.

Briscoe, C. W. and J. B. Smith. "Psychiatric illness—marital units and divorce." *The Journal of Nervous and Mental Disease* 158:440-445, 1974.

Brown, Carol A., Roslyn Feldberg, E. M. Fox and J. Kohen. "Divorce: Chance of a new lifetime." *Journal of Social Issues* 32:119-133, 1976.

Brown, Prudence, Barbara J. Felton, Victor Whiteman, and Roger Manela. "Attachment and distress following marital separation." *Journal of Divorce* 3:303-317, 1980.

Burchinal, L. G. "Characteristics of adolescents from unbroken, broken, and reconstituted families." *Journal of Marriage and Family* 26:44-51, 1964.

Carter H. and P. C. Glick. *Marriage and divorce: A social and economic study.* Cambridge, Mass.: Harvard University Press, 1970.

Cassel, J. "The contribution of the social environment to host resistance." *American Journal of Epidemiology* 104:107-123, 1976.

Chiriboga, David A., Ann Coho, Judith A. Stein, and John Roberts. "Divorce, stress and social supports: A study in helpseeking behavior." *Journal of Divorce* 3:121-135, 1979.

Cobb, S. "Social Support as a moderator of life stress." *Psychosomatic Medicine* 38:301-314, 1976.

Colletta, N. D., "Support systems after divorce: Incidence and impact." *Journal of Marriage and the Family* 41:837-846, 1979. (a)

Colletta, N. D. "The impact of divorce: Father absence or poverty?" *Journal of Divorce* 3:27-35, 1979. (b)

Dell, P. F. and A. S. Appelbaum. "Trigenerational enmeshment: Unresolved ties of single-parents to family of origin." *American Journal of Orthopsychiatry* 47:52-59, 1977.

Earls, Felton and Ben Siegel. "Precocious fathers." *American Journal of Orthopsychiatry* 50:469-480, 1980.

Espenshade, Thomas J. "The economic consequences of divorce." *Journal of Marriage and the Family* 41(3):615-625, 1979.

Fox, John W. "Gove's specific sex-role theory of mental illness: A research note." *Journal of Health and Social Behavior* 21:260-267, 1980.

Furstenberg Jr., Frank F. and Kathy Gordon Talvitie. "Children's names and paternal claims: Bonds between unmarried fathers and their children." *Journal of Family Issues* 1:31-57, 1980.

Glasser, Paul and Elizabeth Navarre. "Structural problems of the one-parent family." Pp. 83–90 In M. B. Sussman (Ed.), *Sourcebook in Marriage and the Family* (4th edition). Boston: Houghton-Mifflin Company, 1974.

Goetting, Ann. "Former spouse—Current spouse relationships. *Journal of Family Issues* 1:58-80, 1980.

Goldsmith, Jean. *Relationships between former spouses: Descriptive findings.* Revision of paper presented at the meeting of the National Council on Family Relations, Boston, 1979.

Gongla, Patricia A. *Social relationships after marital separation: A study of women with children.* Unpublished doctoral dissertation, Case Western Reserve University, 1977.

Gongla, Patricia A. *Single parent families: Extended and extra-familial aid and the socialization of children.* Paper presented at the meeting of the Society for the Study of Social Problems, Montreal, 1974.

Goode, William J. *Women in Divorce*. New York: The Free Press, 1956.

Gove, W. R. "Sex, marital status and suicide." *Journal of Health and Social Behavior* 13:204-213, 1972.

Greenberg, Judith B. "Single parenting and intimacy. A comparison of mothers and fathers." *Alternative Lifestyles* 2:308-330, 1979.

Grow, Lucille J. "Today's unmarried mothers: The choices have changed." *Child Welfare* 58:363-371, 1979.

Hartnagel, Timothy F. "Father absence and self-conception among lower class white and Negro boys. *Social Problems* 18:152-163, 1970.

Herzog, Elizabeth and Cecelia E. Sudia. "Boys in fatherless families." Washington, D.C.: U.S. DHEW Office of Child Development, 1970.

Herzog, Elizabeth and Cecelia E. Sudia. "Fatherless homes: A review of research." *Children* 15:177-182, 1968.

Heatherington, E. Mavis. "Effects of father absence on personality development in adolescent daughters." *Developmental Psychology* 7:313-326, 1972.

Heatherington, E. Mavis. "Girls without fathers." *Psychology Today* 47:49-52, 1973.

Heatherington, E. Mavis, Martha Cox and Roger Cox. "The aftermath of divorce." In J. H. Stevens, Jr. and Marilyn Mathews (Eds.), *Mother-Child, Father-Child Relations*. Washington, D.C.: NAEYC, 1977.

Heatherington, E. Mavis, Martha Cox and Roger Cox. "The development of children in mother-headed families." Pp. 117–145 In David Reiss and Howard A. Hoffman (Eds.), *The American Family: Dying or Developing*. New York: The Plenum Press, 1979.

Heatherington, E. Mavis and Jan L. Deur. "The effects of father absence on child development." *Young Children* 26:233-248, 1971.

Hiltz, Starr Roxanne. "Widowhood: A roleless role." *Marriage and Family Review* 1:1-10, 1978.

Hoffman, Martin L. "Father absence and conscience development." *Developmental Psychology* 4:400-406, 1971.

Hoffman, S. "Marital instability and the economic status of women." *Demography* 14:67-76, 1977.

Hunt, L. L. and Hunt, J. G., "Race and the father-son connection: The conditional relevance of father absence for the orientations and identities of adolescent boys." *Social Problems* 23:35-52, 1975.

Hunt, M. and Hunt, B. *The Divorce Experience*. San Francisco: McGraw-Hill, 1977.

Jacobson, Doris S. "The impact of marital separation/divorce on children: II. Interparent hostility and child adjustment." *Journal of Divorce* 2:3-19, 1978.

Kalter, N. "Children of divorce in an outpatient psychiatric population." *American Journal of Orthopsychiatry* 47:40-51, 1977.

Kessler, Ronald C. "Stress, social status, and psychological distress." *Journal of Health and Social Behavior* 20:259-272, 1979.

Kitson, Gay C., Helena Znaniecka Lopata, William M. Holmes, Suzanne M. Meyering. "Divorces and widows: Similarities and differences." *American Journal of Orthopsychiatry* 50:291-301, 1980.

Kriesberg, Louis. *Mothers in Poverty*. Chicago: Aldine Publishing Co., 1970.

Kurdek, Lawrence and Albert E. Siesky, Jr. "Sex role self-concepts of single divorced parents and their children." *Journal of Divorce* 3:249-261, 1980.

Lamb, Michael. "The effects of divorce on children's personality development." *Journal of Divorce* 1:163-174, 1977.

Landis, J. T. "The trauma of children when parents divorce." *Marriage and Family Living* 22:7-16, 1960.

Lessing, Elise E., Susan W. Zagorin, and Dorothy Nelson. "WISC subtest and IQ score correlates of father absence." *The Journal of Genetic Psychology* 117:181-195, 1970.

Lester, D., and A. T. Beck. "Early loss as a possible 'sensitizer' to later loss in attempted suicides." *Psychological Reports* 39:121-122, 1976.

Liebow, Elliot. *Tally's Corner*. Boston: Little, Brown, 1967.

Loge, B. J. "Role adjustments to single parenthood: A study of divorced and widowed men and women." *Dissertation Abstracts International* 4647A, 1977.

Longabaugh, R. "Mother behavior as a variable moderating the effects of father absence." *Ethos* 1:456-465, 1973.

Magreb, Phyllis R. "For the sake of the children: A review of the psychological effects of divorce." *Journal of Divorce* 1:233-245, 1978.

Mallan, L. B. "Young widows and their children: A comparative report." *Social Security Bulletin* 38:3-21, 1975.

McCord, J., W. McCord, and E. Thurber. "Some effects of paternal absence on male children." *Journal of Abnormal and Social Psychology* 64:361-369, 1962.

McCubbin, Hamilton and Pauline Grossenbacher Boss. "Family stress and coping: Targets for theory, research, counseling, and education." *Family Relations* 29:429-444, 1980.

Mueller, Daniel P. "Social networks: A promising direction for research on the relationship of the social environment to psychiatric disorder." *Social Science and Medicine* 14A:147-161, 1980.

Nelsen, Edward A. and Patricia M. Vangen. "Impact of father absence on heterosexual behaviors and social development of preadolescent girls in a ghetto environment." *Proceedings of the 79th Annual Convention of the American Psychological Association* 6:165-166, 1971.

Nye, F. Ivan. "Child adjustment in broken and unhappy unbroken homes." *Marriage and Family Living* 19:356-361, 1957.

O'Brien, David J. and T. Neal Garland. *Bridging the gap between theory, research, practice, and policy-making: The case of interaction with kin after divorce.* Paper presented at the annual meeting of the National Council on Family Relations, San Diego, 1977.

Parker, Seymour and Robert J. Kleiner. "Characteristics of Negro mothers in single-headed households." *Journal of Marriage and the Family* 28:507-513, 1966.

Pearlin, L. I. and J. S. Johnson. "Marital status, life-strains and depression." *American Sociological Review* 42:704-715, 1977.

Phelps, David W. "Parental attitudes toward family life and child behavior of mothers in two-parent and one-parent families." *The Journal of School Health* 34:413-416, 1969.

Pipher, M. D. "The effects of father absence on the sexual development and adjustment of adolescent daughters and their mothers." *Dissertation Abstracts International* 913B, 1977.

Presser, Harriet B. *Sally's Corner: Coping with unmarried motherhood.* Paper presented at the meeting of the American Sociological Association, San Francisco, 1978.

Raschke, Helen J. and Vernon J. Raschke. "Family conflict and children's self-concepts: A comparison of intact and single-parent families. *Journal of Marriage and the Family* 41:367-374, 1979.

Rasmussen, D. D. "Sex role differentiation in one-parent families." *Dissertation Abstracts International* 5624B, 1975.

Renne, Karen S. "Health and marital experience in an urban population." *Journal of Marriage and the Family* 33:338-350, 1971.

Rico-Velasco, J. and L. Mynko. "Suicide and marital status: A changing relationship? *Journal of Marriage and the Family* 35:239-244, 1973.

Rosen, Rhona, "Some crucial issues concerning children of divorce." *Journal of Divorce* 3:19-25, 1979.

Rosenfeld, Jona M. and Eliezer Rosenstein. "Towards a comceptual framework for the study of parent-absent families." *Journal of Marriage and the Family* 35:131-135, 1973.

Ross, Heather L. and Isabel V. Sawhill. *Time of Transition: The Growth of Families Headed by Women*. Washington, D.C.: The Urban Institute, 1975.

Santrock, John W. "Effects of father absence on sex-typed behaviors in male children:

Reason for the absence and age of onset of the absence." *The Journal of Genetic Psychology* 130:3-10, 1977.

Santrock, John W. "Relation of type and onset of father absence to cognitive development." *Child Development* 43:455-469, 1972.

Shorr, Alvin L. and Phyllis Moen. "The single parent and public policy." *Social Policy* 9:15-21, 1979.

Sibbison, V. H. *Pennsylvania's female-headed households: Families in Distress.* University Park, Pennsylvania: Institute for the Study of Human Development, Pennsylvania State University, 1974.

Smith, Michael J. "The social consequences of single parenthood: A longitudinal perspective." *Family Relations* 29:75-81, 1980.

Spicer, Jerry W. and Gary D. Hampe. "Kinship interaction after divorce." *Journal of Marriage and the Family* 37:113-119, 1975.

Sprey, Jetse. "Conflict theory and the study of marriage and the family." Pp. 130–159 In Wesley R. Burr, Reuben Hill, F. Ivan Nye, Ira L. Reiss (Eds.), *Contemporary Theories about the Family, Volume II.* New York: The Free Press, 1979.

Stack, Carol B. *All Our Kin: Strategies for Survival in a Black Community.* New York: Harper and Row, Publishers, 1974.

Stein, R. L. "The economic status of families headed by women." *Monthly Labor Review* 93:3-10, 1970.

St. Pierre, Maurice. *Black female single parent family: A preliminary sociological perspective.* Paper presented at the meeting of the American Sociological Association, New York, 1980.

Sweet, James A. "The living arrangements of separated, widowed and divorced mothers." *Demography* 9:143-157, 1972.

The Consortium for the Study of Schools Needs of Children from One-Parent Families. *The most significant minority; One-parent children in the schools.* The National Association of Elementary School Principals and the Institute for Development of Educational Activities, Arlington, Virginia, 1980.

Turner, R. Jay. *Experienced social support as a contingency in emotional well-being.* Paper presented at the meeting of the American Sociological Association, New York, 1980.

U.S. Bureau of the Census. *Statistical Abstract of the United States: 1979* (100th Edition). Washington, D.C., 1979.

U.S. Bureau of the Census. "Marital Status and Living Arrangements: March, 1979." *Current Population Reports* Series P-20, No. 349, 1980.

Verbrugge, Louis M. "Marital Status and health." *Journal of Marriage and the Family* 41(2)-:267-285, 1979.

Vincent, C. E. *Unmarried Mothers.* New York: The Free Press, 1961.

Wallerstein, Judith and Joan B. Kelly. "The effect of parental divorce: Experiences of the preschool child." *Journal of American Academy of Child Psychiatry* 14:600-616, 1975.

Wallerstein, Judith and Joan B. Kelly. "The effect of parental divorce: Experiences of the child in later latency." *American Journal of Orthopsychiatry* 46:256-269, 1976.

Wallerstein, Judith and Joan B. Kelly. "Children and divorce: A review." *Social Work* 24:468-475.

Wallerstein, Judith and Joan B. Kelly. *Surviving the Breakup: How Children and Parents Cope with Divorce.* New York: Basic Books, 1980.

Wattenberg, Esther and Hazel Reinhardt. "Female-headed families: Trends and implications." *Social Work* 24:460-467, 1979.

Weiss, Robert S. *Marital Separation.* New York: Basic Books, Inc., 1975.

Weiss, Robert S. *Going It Alone: The Family Life and Social Situation of the Single Parent.* New York: Basic Books, Inc., 1979.

Wohlford, Paul, John W. Santrock, Stephen E. Berger, and David Liberman. "Older brothers' influence on sex-typed aggressive and dependent behavior in father-absent children." *Developmental Psychology* 4:124-134, 1971.

Woolsey, Suzanne, H. "Pied Piper politics and the child-care debate." *Daedulus* 106:127-145, 1977.

Zold, A. C. "The effects of father absence during childhood on later adjustment: A long-term follow-up. *Dissertation Abstracts International* 164B, 1975.

FAMILY IN THE KIBBUTZ:
A REVIEW OF AUTHORITY RELATIONS
AND WOMEN'S STATUS

Rosanna Hertz

The kibbutz system in Israel has presented social scientists of all ideological stripes with a unique and perplexing situation: the kibbutz stands as a seventy year old social experiment[1] which has provided tremendous opportunities for understanding social life but which, at the same time, has led to the creation of competing, conflicting and often contradictory theories of the same phenomenon. Any review of research and findings on the kibbutz will necessarily reproduce some measure of this dilemma.

This essay will focus on two connected facets of kibbutz social structure which have drawn considerable attention from researchers, kibbutz specialists and the knowledgeable public. The first deals directly with the structure and emergence of family in the kibbutz. This is important because the institution of family was altered in kibbutz life. I will focus on the position of family in kibbutzim and the larger implications of family for community and control. Does family operate as a competing or complementary authority structure in the community? Has the family produced a system of political inequality in an economically egalitarian community?

The second facet of kibbutz social structure I will consider is the status of women. This issue has superseded concerns with family organization in recent years. Competing explanations for the contemporary status of kibbutz women will be reviewed. Here, the kibbutz as an ongoing social experiment has provided fertile grounds for determining whether sex roles are socially constructed or biologically determined.

Ms. Hertz is a Ph.D. candidate and a Lecturer in Sociology at Northwestern University, Evanston, IL. This paper benefited greatly from the advice and criticism of Robert Thomas. Special thanks also to Joy Charlton, Janet Lever, Allan Schnaiberg, Christopher Jencks Zelda Gamson, William Gamson, David Rubinstein and Steve Warner.

Family and Community

Researchers in the 1950's and 1960's debated both the existence and form of family organization in the kibbutz. In the last ten years, however, researchers have generally agreed that family has become a stable feature. Spiro, for example, initially concluded in his early works (1954; 1960) that the collective superceded kin in the economic, educational and social spheres of kibbutz life. In effect, the family did not exist. However, in his most recent book he concedes that family has become a significant phenomenon in the kibbutz (Spiro, 1979). Stimulus for the recognition of family has come from historical change in the kibbutz itself. Groups have emerged which fulfill definitional criteria for family (e.g., Murdock, 1949:1), and those groups have organized themselves into publicly proclaimed family and kin groupings displaying cohesion around blood and kin ties.

More problematic, and a topic of disagreement among researchers, is the position of the family in the communal-social structure and the role family plays in the kibbutz authority system. These areas of inquiry provide the most useful focus for reviewing social science investigations on the kibbutz family.[2] To make this review useful to those not familiar with kibbutz research, I will merge historical material with the research and theory developed in the past three decades.[3]

Family in the Early Kibbutz

During the first stage of kibbutz development, called the "revolutionary" (Talmon, 1972) or "pioneering" (Blumberg, 1974) phase, family and kinship barely existed and thus did not pose immediate ideological or structural problems. Blood ties were few among Eastern European immigrants who had severed ties with family and kin to travel to Palestine to establish kibbutzim. Men outnumbered women, with the latter accounting for at most one-third of the total kibbutz membership in the 1920's and 1930's. The population grew largely by immigration, rather than by natural increase (Talmon, 1972).

The demographic composition of the immigrant population—particularly the sex ratio imbalance—was one factor in subordinating the position of the family in the early kibbutz. Talmon (1972:4-7), however, suggests three additional factors suppressed the development of family. First, the powerful revolutionary Socialist-Zionist ideology which fueled the kibbutz movement and attracted young immigrants also infused members with a strong communal purpose. The appeal of the ideology crosscut family and community in Europe and, as a result, was one of the few common elements uniting new members with one another and with movement "veterans."[4] Beyond a powerful ideology, however, kibbutz members believed they occupied an important position in the future Jewish-Israeli state: the nation would be formed through the kibbutz as generations of new citizens would be trained in the communal settlements. In other words, the kibbutz would represent Israel's ideological birthplace and its revolutionary conscience. The primacy of ideology, as a unifying factor and as a link to Israel's potential future, overshadowed other forms of commitment. Hence, family ties and family development were subordinated in favor of communal ties and communal development. As Talmon (1972:13) notes, family was subordinated although never completely abolished:

> It should be noted that although the kibbutzim limited the functions of the family drastically, they did not abolish it altogether. Nor was the antifamilistic policy in the kibbutz based on a preconceived or fully worked out ideology. Most early formation of ideological position did not propose to do away with the family.

The second factor directly impinging on family development was the economic organization of the kibbutz. Lacking sufficient capital, machinery and labor, the kibbutz channeled most of its resources into agricultural production and kept services minimal. In line with their organizational ideology, members established a communal division of labor, and the harsh living conditions reinforced the maximal obligation of individuals to the group. Talmon (1972:5), referring to the economic situation of the kibbutz, concludes: "The nonfamilistic division of labor was to a large extent a matter of economic necessity."

The third limit on family was the role the kibbutz played in regional and national defense (Talmon, 1972:4-5). Many kibbutzim were (and are today) defense outposts. The real or potential threat to the kibbutz and to the state strengthened communal attachments, and the communal division of labor facilitated the rapid conversion from agricultural settlement to semi-military garrison.

Thus, the "underdevelopment" of the family in the early years of the kibbutz can be understood as the outcome of a variety of factors: demographic, ideological, economic and military/political. As Talmon showed quite convincingly, these factors were far more important than a rigorously anti-familistic ideology in the kibbutz.

However, what is perhaps underemphasized in Talmon's (and other's) work is an important organizational correlate of family: competing bases for authority in the community. While the demographic, economic and military/political conditions discussed above certainly made survival tenuous for kibbutzim, those conditions had historically confronted other settlements (e.g., frontier settlements in the American west, early waves of colonization). What distinguished the kibbutzim was their reliance on an egalitarian ideology as a basis for mobilization and control. Under conditions of tenuous economic and political survival, the emphasis on community before family made it possible to exploit meager resources as well as to rapidly mobilize labor for production and arms for defense. The existence of intervening authority structures, e.g., father over wife and children might have compromised the ability of the collective's leaders to effectively mobilize members. Also, mobilization would be impaired if there were disputes in the definition of family and collective interests.

Family was not the only alternative basis of authority. Religious authority was also curtailed and the power of rabbis severely limited (cf. Spiro, 1963). Status honor groups derived from formal education, professions and crafts, and prior wealth were explicitly de-valued and efforts were made to prevent their reemergence as power centers.

The family in the early stage of the kibbutz, therefore, was not explicitly targeted for "destruction," as is often assumed. Rather, family development was limited by the interaction of historical, ideological and economic factors with the suspicion of family as a competing locus of loyalty. Some factions within the kibbutz movement may have opposed family formation on broader principles. However, the ideology was not monolithic and historical circumstances played a more important role.

The Dyad: How Family Emerged

While family was not initially important to population growth and was suspect as an alternative authority structure, it did represent one solution to a pressing problem in the kibbutz: intimacy. The need for intimacy and privacy in social and sexual relations was recognized by kibbutz members (Spiro, 1954; 1960). But, the mechanisms by which intimacy was to be achieved were problematic. How could the collective sanction intimacy without allowing the form in which it would be fostered to develop into an alternative and perhaps more powerful basis of allegiance among kibbutz members?

Originally, the collective sought to substitute community for family as the provider of intimacy: ". . . the sentiments of love, affection and cooperation, which traditionally were associated with family, were to be transferred to the collectivity" (Spiro, 1979:11). However, the practice of "community as family" suffered from two major obstacles. First, as Spiro (1954:846) noted in an early work, community as family is limited by population size. To the extent that population growth limits the amount and quality of face-to-face interactions, the capacity of the collective to substitute for family diminishes.[5] Second, the intensity of interactions among kibbutz members acted to overpower individuals. That is, every aspect of communal life was subject to intense scrutiny and debate in work and non-work settings as well as formal meetings (cf. Spiro, 1963:92-93). Thus, the all-embracing character of kibbutz life pushed many members to seek refuge in intimate relationships. Talmon (1972:13) observes: "by providing unconditional love and loyalty, [the family] insulated its members from communal pressures and enhanced their security."

In response to the collectives' inability to provide intimacy (particularly as they grew larger and more complex) and to the need for protection from communal pressure, the dyadic relationship developed. Pairs of men and women, drawn together as close friends or as lovers, were tolerated by the kibbutz. Given general, though diffuse, sentiments against the traditional family and the potential for alternative sources of allegiance, the dyad was allowed as a social relationship subordinate to that of membership in the collective. As Talmon (1956:256-7) described:

> Premarital relations were considered legitimate and not censored. . . . Marriage was to be a voluntary union between free persons and was not to be binding on the marital partners only as long as it continued to be based on sincere and deep attachment and as long as both partners wanted it.

Sanctioning the creation of a family-like organization for the purpose of providing intimacy did not, however, simultaneously sanction the development of a durable social organization. What was sanctioned was the development of a *non-reproducible* social relationship: the "lover" relationship. Sexual freedom was encouraged[6] precisely because it would not lead to the development of durable social organizations and because it discouraged the creation of children, the tie which would bind two people together in a traditional union. The fluidity of the dyadic relationship was further encouraged by a disregard for the legal vows of traditional marriages, an emphasis on discretion and limited public displays of affection between couples, and a refusal to make concessions to couples in terms of scheduling work allocations and shifts (cf. Talmon, 1956:256–8).

The Rise of Familism

The tension between collective life and privacy increased as dyadic relationships produced offspring. The kibbutz sought to limit the family to child-production and intimacy by strictly separating economic production and family life. The result has been, according to recent research, an increasing identification of community with production and family with consumption (cf. Gerson, 1978).

In the early years, as Talmon notes, the collective grudgingly gave ground to stable, child-producing dyads: "The formal wedding was usually delayed until the birth of the first child, and was performed mainly because it was the only way to legitimate children according to the laws of the land" (1956:257). Even then: "Any tendency to stay away in the family rooms and to build up a segregated family life was sharply condemned" (Talmon, 1956:258). Nonetheless, children created a durable social bond between individuals which the community could not entirely replace.[7]

The community itself helped foster these bonds by emphasizing natural population increase as the flow of immigrants dwindled during the 1940's. As movements sought to expand, kibbutzim had to accommodate increased family formation while simultaneously limiting the autonomy of the family unit. The arrangement which developed separated membership in the collective and participation in the collective economy from membership in the family and participation in intimate relations.

Throughout its history, the kibbutz has represented a single economic unit. Members' needs are met through the communal organization of production and consumption. The growth of family did not alter this system. As Gerson (1978:48) has argued, the kibbutz is distinguished by the fact that families are not self-contained economic units. Family members are not dependent upon the economic achievements of a single producer nor of a kin group. Likewise, from the standpoint of the collective, differences in family size or composition (e.g., the number of male children) cannot lead to the development of economic classes in the community.

Although the family has limited autonomy in the sphere of production, it has affected the sphere of consumption—particularly as the kibbutz progressed beyond economic subsistence (cf. Gerson, 1978; Talmon,

1972; Spiro, 1979). As economic surplus increased, consumption levels have also risen and many of the expenditures have been oriented toward family consumption. Thus, the gradual increase in standard of living has been accompanied by greater control of married couples over their own budgets. For example, in contrast to previous single-room dwellings, the contemporary kibbutz home has two rooms, individual kitchen facilities and a private bathroom. Some kibbutzim have also added individual televisions and air conditioners.

The influence of family on consumption patterns does not represent a shift toward familial jurisdiction over the economy. Instead, the shift has been toward greater privacy, perhaps as a means of increasing intimacy among family members. This was first indicated by Talmon in the 1950's as she examined childrens' sleeping and eating arrangements (1972:74-117). In general, she found that kibbutzim which allowed children to sleep in their parents' private quarters (instead of in childrens' houses) placed greater emphasis on family concerns and a higher local standard of living. By contrast, those which maintained separate domiciles for children emphasized a stronger attachment to the communal ideology and national economic goals. Shepher (1969) argued that family influence has spread beyond sleeping and eating arrangements to include family priority in consumption goals. Spiro (1979) found that to reinforce communal dining, some kibbutzim have made substantial investments in improving dining facilities.[8]

The Extended Family: Continuity and Division

Family has become well-engrained in the social structure of the kibbutz over the past three decades. Extended families, encompassing three full generations of kibbutz members, have also come to symbolize both continuity and division in the community (Hertz and Baker, 1980). The extended family, and particularly the cohesive clans, represents the latest phase in the friction between family and community in the kibbutz. That friction has taken on greater significance as extended families have grown sufficiently large to exercise influence over community decision-making.

Many researchers have noted the increasing numerical and organizational importance of extended families. Ichilov and Bar (1980:426), for example, argued that extended families enhance community continuity and stability: ". . . (E)xtended family members do not tend to leave the kibbutz even in kibbutzim that show population decreases." Part of the stabilizing influence of the extended family resides in the creation of kinship sentiments (Gerson, 1978). For example, an individual now belongs to a three generational set of kin relations; reference to one's "family" encompasses aunts, uncles, grandparents, siblings, cousins, children and so on. Furthermore, fictive kinship provides another indication of extended family relations. Couples or individuals joining a collective without resident relatives are quite commonly "adopted" by a host family. Increased ties among family members thus add to the stability of the kibbutz population.[9] Equally important, familial pressure can be used to strengthen the attachment of family members to the kibbutz.

But, as increasing numbers of researchers are finding, the extended family is capable of exercising political influence on the collective as well. At this stage, the aggregate findings are mixed, due in large part to a lack of direct investigation into this issue. However, some researchers have begun to present evidence of increased *political* inequality between extended families. That is, in some kibbutzim, extended families and cohesive clans mediate access to important positions of authority in the community. Thus far, no evidence has been presented to link extended families to economic inequality between individuals or between families. To that extent, the principle of communal distribution of economic resources has not been affected: there are no rich or poor families residing in the same collective.[10]

Except for some of the most recent research (e.g., Ichilov and Bar, 1980; Hertz and Baker, 1980), the interaction between extended family and community has been dealt with only in passing. Nonetheless, other writers provide important clues as to the nature of that interaction. Spiro (1979:41-2) notes that an important structural change has been the institutionalization of the extended family: "(W)ith the growing importance of extended family, there are even signs in some kibbutzim of the development of extended family *households* (emphasis added)."[11] Gerson (1978: 54), in his critique of the familistic trend warns:

> If the extended family is allowed to operate as an organized pressure group in the kibbutz assembly in matters concerning vocational training and placement of one of its members, the result may easily be "hereditary" high status positions of members of a specific clan.

Similarly, Tiger and Shepher (1975:40) note that:

> . . . large families command a new form and degree of solidarity and constitute a potential threat to the political system. A group of

fifteen to twenty-five adults . . . could easily become a power group defending the family's own interests instead of the collective's.

Ichilov and Bar's (1980) study of four veteran kibbutzim explores the relationship between extended family formation and the advancement of family interests in community decision-making and resource allocation. Concentrating on the distribution of positions of authority and positional resources, e.g., cars and access to study outside the kibbutz, they found that members of extended families held a disproportionate share of those positions and resources in two kibbutzim. In the other two kibbutzim, members of extended families enjoyed no clear advantages. Because the two kibbutzim which exhibited some family control differed widely on the extent of extended family membership, however, Ichilov and Bar's findings are not conclusive. Part of the difficulty resides in the inadequacy of appropriate measures of extended family structure, cohesion and influence. Ichilov and Bar's (1980:426) concluding advice is worth repeating:

> . . . One must examine the patterns of organization and operation of extended family in the kibbutz. Also, since families clearly do not operate in a vacuum, especially within the kibbutz, one has to take into account the power structure of the kibbutz itself.

While not providing the comparison which might yield more conclusive results, Hertz and Baker (1980) move in this direction with their case study of another veteran kibbutz. They identify the clan *(hamula)* as a type of extended family characterized by a strong leader (usually a founding member of the kibbutz), considerable cohesion among family members, high levels of intra-family interaction, and consistent expression of family interests. They argue, as do Ichilov and Bar, that extended families (and clans) enhance continuity in kibbutz life. At the same time, they point out that clans are divisive forces with considerable influence in the economic, political and social life of the community. Through a comparison of extended families, Hertz and Baker suggest that the capacity of an extended family to become a clan, and thus exercise some influence in community life, is related to marital patterns, bridges between extended families, and the birthplace of family members. Though these variables are only partially defined, they do open avenues of inquiry into the organization of stronger and weaker extended family units, and to the effect of families on the kibbutz.

Kinship in the present is a complementary authority structure. Kinship was initially suspect because it was seen as a potentially competing authority system and thus a threat to the collective's survival. Family was allowed to emerge in limited form from the beginning, as a provider of intimacy, and family has remained an important means by which intimacy is achieved in kibbutz life. This is not to argue that intimacy in the kibbutz only exists within families, nor to suggest that family is the only organization capable of providing intimacy, e.g., cohorts remain a common basis around which close friendships are formed (cf. Baker and Hertz, 1981). It is to argue, however, that the locus of intimacy was initially the couple and that intimacy became routinized within the family. As a result, the kibbutz became primarily an economic organization and the family became the conduit for expressions of love, sentiment and affection. In the present, the family complements the kibbutz as a stabilizing influence but the extended family may in the future become a competing authority structure with the clan as the locus of political inequality.

The Status of Women: Social Structure or Biology?

In the past decade, sexual equality has become a major focal point for kibbutz research. The status of women in the kibbutz is considered for several reasons. First, kibbutzim and other communal movements have been looked to as possible models for a non-sexist community. Second, as Gerson (1978) and Rosner (1967) have pointed out, kibbutz women themselves have questioned whether they are indeed "equal" with men, especially with respect to the allocation of work roles and occupational prestige.[12] Finally, the kibbutz as an "ongoing social experiment" has provided what some believe to be fertile ground for determining whether sex roles are socially constructed or biologically determined.

Before examining the explanations advanced about women's status in the kibbtuz it is necessary to describe briefly just what is the "problem." Two major aspects of the empirical problem are: (1) differential levels of participation in committee work and political influence by sex, and (2) a high level of sex segregation in labor allocation. That is, women are concentrated in the service sector of the kibbutz, predominantly in the children's houses, the kitchen and the laundry/sewing facilities (non-income generating work). Men are disproportionately represented in agricultural and industrial work, i.e., sectors which generate revenue for the community or "productive" work.[13]

Attempts to explain the relationship between women's status, the rise of family and the division of labor in the kibbutz have generated tremendous controversy.[14] On the one side are the "structuralists," among them Talmon (1972), Blumberg (1977), and Bowes (1978), who argue that changes in the social and economic structure of the kibbutz have created a system of sexual stratification which perpetuates women's low status and family position. On the other side are the "sociobiologists" and "psychobiologists," including Tiger and Shepher (1975), who argue that women's contemporary position represents the emergence of their biologically and psychologically engrained predispositions. Spiro (1979) is more difficult to categorize in these terms, because he does lend weight to historical change but also asserts the importance of "pre-cultural" dispositional variables.

Equality between the Sexes: Early Stages

Sexual equality in the early kibbutz was expressed in a particularly male fashion: male work activities and qualities were seen as the ideal for both sexes. Women's adoption of this masculine-role prototype has been documented by a wide range of researchers (cf. Talmon, 1972; Blumberg, 1974; Bowes, 1978; Gerson, 1978; Spiro, 1979). The question which requires explanation, however, is why women adhered to a male prototype. Were they attempting to shed a psychological or biological predisposition toward "female" behavior? Were they responding to the needs of the community? Were they attempting to achieve truly equal status with men?

Different authors have provided their own interpretations of women and the male prototype. Spiro (1963:230), working in the fields alongside men and women, observed that "women work longer than men, remaining in the fields beyond quitting time . . . and that, in general, they work at a harder pace than do the men, who work more leisurely." He concludes: "Hence, even those women who have achieved economic 'emancipation' are still not 'emancipated' psychologically" (1963:230). To Spiro, women were not better or more responsible workers than men; instead, they had to overcome a psychological handicap.

From a structuralist perspective, by contrast, Talmon (1972:7) suggests that adherence to the masculine prototype was a preventive measure:

> The emphasis was on activities outside the family orbit and the masculine-role prototype prevented an intense identification with the role of mother, and curbed the desire for children.

Whether the "desire for children" represented a biological drive in Talmon's argument is unclear; however, identification with the male prototype provided a hedge against the development of traditional sex roles. Finally, Bowes (1978:242) suggests that women's behavior was purposive with respect to women's status: ". . . certain women were *fighting for a place* in what they saw as a male dominated movement: the places they wanted were alongside the men, performing the same tasks (emphasis added." In other words, women worked harder in order to prove their equality and to cement equal status.

A similar split occurs in attempts to explain why women adopted male attire. Spiro argues that women again sought to compensate for inner drives:

> Indeed, for the pioneer women any kind of sexual differentiation—including sexual dimorphism—was viewed as a symbol of female inferiority, and hence was to be minimized as far as possible. . . . To be equals of men, women were to become like men not only in their occupational roles, but in their external appearance as well. It was as if the women felt that to achieve equality with men, they had to reject their femininity (1979:8-9).

Talmon (1956:256-7), however, argues that because of the unequal ratio of men to women in the kibbutz, restraint and moderation toward sex was important. This demographic disequilibrium, as she terms it, resulted in competition and shifting sex roles, on the one hand, and "deep-seated asceticism," on the other. Therefore, women dressing like men served as a mechanism by which the kibbutz attempted to control sexuality. Talmon argued:

> the kibbutz developed many ingenious mechanisms which toned it [sexual attraction] down and checked its disorganizing effects. Relations between the sexes were de-eroticized and neutralized by dealing with sexual problems in a straightforward, objective and 'rational' manner and by minimizing the differentiation and distance between the sexes. Women adopted male style of dress and patterns of behavior. Beauty care and personal adornment which played up and enhanced feminity were completely eliminated.

Hence, women were not necessarily rejecting "being women"; their sexuality was being downplayed for the purposes of the collective. Finally, Bowes (1978:244) suggests another interpretation:

"Egalitarianism" in the movement was asymmetrical, in that the women were taking on what had traditionally been men's jobs and they were involved in a feminist struggle in addition to the Socialist Zionist struggle. Men were not taking on women's traditional roles and they did not conceive of changes in the position of women beyond their entering the "male world" of work.

According to Bowes, women were working in the "productive" branches not only because of economic necessity, but also because work alone was not enough to advance equality. To cement their work lives as permanent, women further adopted male qualities.

In light of the lack of substantive historical or longitudinal data on women, the debate among researchers might be dismissed as indeterminate. However, this debate is critical because this experiment has been widely utilized in generating more general theories of sex role behavior. Interpretations of this stage, and subsequent developments discussed below, have been used by Tiger and Shepher (1975) and Spiro (1979) to develop a theory of biological and/or precultural imperatives. If women's adherence to a male model failed to overcome the biological determination of behavior, then that failure suggests the intervening period simply represented the reemergence of biological imperatives. But, if women's adherence to the male model represented a strategy to create and defend sexual equality, then it is important to investigate what sociological variables or processes undermined the development of a durable structure of sexual equality.

Later Stages

As the economic situation of most kibbutzim improved beyond subsistence, the birth rate increased considerably (Talmon, 1965:271-2; Gerson, 1978:570). Furthermore, as the flow of immigrants declined kibbutz births came to represent an important source of population increase. Baratz (1956:72-73) notes that with the first births in one of the initial kibbutzim, Degania, the question of childcare became an issue. Since childcare was not regarded as productive labor, the question was, more appropriately, who shall *not* rear the children? While the development of children's houses was consistent with the communal ideology of the kibbutz, it was also economically necessary (Talmon, 1972:8). That is, the children's houses minimized the labor devoted to non-productive pursuits. Yet, women were the ones assigned to the tasks of childrearing and education: men were never sent to the children's houses (Gerson,

1978; Rabin, 1970; Blumberg, 1977). Why were women selected for this work?

Blumberg (1977), presenting a social structural explanation, argues that despite their adherence to male prototypes women were pushed out of productive work and into the service sector. In assessing kibbutz development up to the end of the pioneering period (late 1930s), she cites two major factors important in determining the nature of that shift. First, and most generally, Blumberg (1977:426) suggests that the kibbutz's "techno-economic base" in agricultural production conflicted with women's biological role as mothers. In particular, most kibbutzim grew crops on the outskirts of the collective. This, however, conflicted with a community emphasis on breastfeeding and frequent contact between mother and child. The result was considerable time lost while women made frequent trips between the (often) distant fields and the children's houses. To resolve this dilemma, Blumberg (1977:425) suggests, women sought to expand horticultural production much closer to the nurseries in order to continue employing mothers as productive laborers.

Two factors undermined a shift to more intensive horticulture. First, according to the kibbutz accounting system, horticulture was less profitable than agriculture. Second, the continued in-flow of male immigrants enabled the kibbutz to gradually replace women in agriculture and, thus, to enhance the development of the children's houses and other services. Without the availability of an external labor source, Blumberg (1977:426) suggests, the erosion of women's employment in agriculture would have been difficult.[15]

In an argument which dovetails with Blumberg's, Talmon contended that the traditional reproductive function of the family which had laid dormant during the early kibbutz years was re-activated and became the basis for the consolidation of family in the social structure *and* the emergence of a feminine role prototype:

> The emergence of a more feminine role prototype for women and the partial emancipation of the family reinforce the tendency for a higher birth rate. It is felt that children consolidate the position of family in the community and contribute to a richer and more varied family life (1956:272).

In other words, women were actively enmeshed in the development of family as a cohesive element in social structure and as an expression of a non-masculine role prototype. At the same time, as women were engaged in the long-term reproduction of the family and the kibbutz labor force, however, they were being disengaged from the productive sector of employment. As the kibbutz invested more and more of its surplus into development of the children's houses and collective education, women were more firmly cemented into positions in the service sector. The creation of childcare training programs and the recruitment of young women as childcare workers further reinforced service occupations as women's work.

Further, researchers present collective education as "beneficial to women." That is, because children are not raised individually women are freed to work full-time. However, Bowes (1978:247) contends that collective education is not enough to emancipate women. Instead, the differential evaluation of work in the kibbutz is critical to women's status.

The differential prestige of agricultural (and later, industrial) sectors and service sectors was derived from the valuation placed by the kibbutz on income-generating production. Even in light of a predominantly socialist ideology, an increasing rate of economic surplus and an equal sharing in the fruits of communal production, higher prestige was and has been devoted to income-generating work.

This can be explained in part as a carry-over from the days of tenuous economic subsistence, but, at the same time, it bespeaks of a generalization of traditional sex roles. Instead of men acquiring their dominance over women via authority relations in the family, men acquired dominance over women via the division of labor in the community. In other words, the dependence of the service sector on the productive sector substitutes for the dependence of wives on husbands. And, since prestige is accorded to one's occupation, women's lower status in the community is mediated by their employment in the service sector and rationalized by stereotypes.

Thus, Rosner found that a majority cited traditional stereotypes, namely feminine traits (e.g., patience, sensitivity) and physical traits (e.g., strength), as determining suitability of women and men for work in the service or production sector, respectively. "The mentioning of these qualities represented, perhaps, not only an explanation of the existing situation but also provided a certain legitimation for it" (1976:83). Women employed in the services, he further argues, experience "a sense of deprivation" given the low prestige of this sector (1976:87).

By contrast with the structuralists, Tiger and Shepher (1975) contend that sex role differences are the product of biological differences, not social division of labor. According to Tiger and Shepher (1975:272), women have:

> acted against the principles of their socialization and ideology, against the wishes of the men in their communities, against the economic interests of the kibbutzim, in order to be able to devote much time and energy to private maternal activities rather than to economic and political ones.

Women's status in the kibbutz is not, therefore, derived from a complex authority or stratification system, but from "a rather sudden change in behavior and a reversal of basic socialization" at the beginning of their reproductive lives (1975:181). This sudden change has its source in what Tiger and Fox (1971) refer to as "biologically determined dispositions" or "biogrammars." Efforts to turn off biogrammars may be successful temporarily, as Tiger and Shepher concede in light of early kibbutz history, but "not for long and not for many people, without causing serious difficulties for the individual and society" (1975:265). Thus, as Tiger and Shepher conclude, women's present status is not so much the outcome of social and economic change as it is the struggle of women to realize their full female selves:

> . . . insofar as women are dissatisfied in the kibbutz, it is not principally because of a polarized sexual division of labor and politics and an oppressive familism as it so clearly is elsewhere. Rather, it is because familism does not yet provide women with as much "feminine" activity and family life as they desire (1975: 259).

Not surprisingly, these arguments have provoked considerable controversy, particularly in light of the disputes over other works on sociobiology (cf. Wilson, 1975). The controversy is heated even further by Tiger and his associates' claims that they can use sociobiology to explain why traditional sex roles have re-emerged in a setting ostensibly hostile to their existence.

Tiger and Shepher do not provide direct evidence for the effects of "biogrammars"; however, they dismiss alternative explanations as insufficient. "Biogrammar" is, therefore, a "logical" residual. Without having provided either positive evidence for the existence of biogrammars or a theory of their operation, we are left with a "black box" explanation whose very impenetrability makes it an extremely unproductive analytic device.

Gerson (1978) also challenges Tiger and Shepher's assumption that parental influence on sex role stereotypes is insignificant. According to Tiger and Shepher (1975:166), early socialization disregards sex differences. Children, they admit, become aware of the sexual division of labor during the time they spend with parents and relatives, but "sex typing in parents' homes is still less than in individualistic socialization: childcare is very egalitarian." Gerson argues that "kibbutz education creates two centers in the life of the child—the parent's home and the children's house" (1978:21). Further, Gerson (1978:35-37) uses his earlier research on women's attitudes to shed light on the "sudden change" in behavior the sociobiologists attach to sexual maturation. In a large-scale study of girls between the ages of 13 and 18 in two kibbutzim, Gerson found that those young women clearly preferred agricultural work over the children's houses. Further, "when asked if women had achieved full equality with men the answers became increasingly negative as the respondents increased with age." Gerson interprets this as showing that:

> . . . as girls grow and become increasingly familiar with and aware of the realities of life in the kibbutz, they are influenced by these realities far more strongly than by ideological teachings . . . where their mothers rebelled against a social system and within it against traditional sex roles and struggles with inner conflicts and disappointments, the younger generation has been raised under conditions in which a differential order of sex roles prevails. Many of them accept these conditions as unchangeable (1978:36).

What Tiger and associates see as the effect of biogrammars, therefore, Gerson describes as the effect of a durable social division of labor reinforced by sexual stereotypes.

Spiro, in his latest work (1979), attempts to bridge the gap between the structuralists and the sociobiologists. In the contemporary kibbutz, he suggests, "equivalence" has superseded "identity" in defining sexual equality (1979:7). In other words, where the early kibbutz was typified by an identity of attributes and behaviors among men and women, the present kibbutz is characterized by equivalence in value placed on male and female attributes and behaviors. Men and women thus exhibit separate but equal attributes and are connected by a "pluralistic system of values" (1979:7). Equally important for Spiro, the sectors in which men and women work are equally valued by the community, thus reinforcing general sexual equivalence.

The formulation raises two issues. First, in asserting a separate but equal status for men and women, he downplays sex-linked status differences in both the work individuals perform and in the positions they occupy in the community. That is, in order for Spiro to deny inequality he must suggest that all work and all workers are equally valued by the community. Yet, as Gerson (1978), Bowes (1978), Rosner (1976) and others have pointed out, there is considerable difference in prestige between work sectors, as well as differences in the participation (and, presumably influence) of men and women in committee work. Second, Spiro separates the history of women in the kibbutz into two periods: the "feminist revolution" and the "feminine counterrevolution" (1979:44). This is his way of distinguishing between women's early and later status in work and community. The latter period, he suggests, represents a resurgence of "pre-cultural motivational positions," i.e., the historically suppressed but ultimately victorious emergence of maternal and familial instincts among women. The feminine counterrevolution thus closely resembles Tiger and Shepher's theory of social change. The problem with Spiro's theory, as with Tiger and Shepher's, is that it tends to deny most of what is "social" about social organization and social change. That is, the constitution of women as a lesser privileged stratum in the community makes it possible for them to be concentrated in a segment of the occupational structure which is valued less in terms of its contribution to the community. The manner in which positions in the kibbutz economy are filled is the focus of my argument. The inequality in status between men and women may be explained or justified on the basis of the presumed biological determination of behavior. But such explanations act only to obscure the bases of inequality (e.g., mechanisms of control for entry into a branch, the differential experience of high school boys and girls). This is clearly not to deny the importance of biology and psychology in social relations; but, at the same time, the reduction of social structure to biology underestimates the real contribution of human beings to history. And while kibbutz women may be seeking traditional feminine roles, to reduce the issues that have produced this quest to biology absolves kibbutzim from responsibility in regard to sexual equality.

Conclusion

Initially, family ties and family development were subordinated in favor of communal ties and community development. However, the community was unable to substitute for family as the provider of intimacy, and thus the revival of the family was rooted in the fulfillment of this need. So, community became synonymous with the economy and family became synonymous with intimacy and privacy. In this regard, kinship presently operates as a complementary system. However, while the community assumed control over economic production, consumption became linked to family. It is in this area that kinship has begun to make inroads as a competing authority system. Future research is needed, both within and between kibbutzim, to determine (1) whether individuals are gaining by forming kinship alliances and what individuals and groups achieve through those alliances (2) how widespread political inequality is between kin groups and (3) whether differential patterns of the allocation of certain resources will eventually lead to the emergence of kinship as the basis of a competing authority system.

In regard to women's status, a gender based division of labor did not develop independent of the economic and ideological life of the community. Therefore the shift in the nature and definition of women's status can be better explained in terms of the growth of the service sector and the removal of women gradually from productive employment. Further, the situation for women was exacerbated as kibbutzim emphasized natural increase. Thus, the biological fact of women's role in reproduction justified the development of a new gender based division of labor. This new division of labor should not draw attention away from the fact that it simultaneously gave rise to certain expected attitudes and behaviors of the different participants in the community, that is sex roles. This is to suggest two important considerations for research on sex roles: first, it is necessary to investigate how economic contingencies can give rise to a gender based division of labor and yet how such a division of labor can be legitimated in terms of communal needs and second, how control over the process of defining and interpreting communal needs is an important factor in establishing and enforcing a gender based division of labor. Thus, the kibbutz will continue to be a uniquely attractive focus of concern, given the struggles which have emerged regarding political and sexual inequality and their bearing on contemporary issues.

NOTES

1. Kibbutzim are collective, socialist settlements located in Israel. There are no specific agenda for the implementation of collective ideology. Instead, even today, solutions are continually found as problems arise. Hence, these collectives are evolving enterprises. In this regard, the kibbutz has been termed a social experiment. The first kibbutz, Degania A, was founded in 1909. However, it was not until the 1920's and 1930's that deliberately large collectives were formed. Today there are 240 kibbutzim, comprising five federations,

with over 100,000 members. Therefore, any paper of this nature suffers from talking about "the kibbutz" or kibbutzim in general.

All kibbutzim share several common features. Initially, they were agricultural settlements, although industry has been gradually introduced since the 1960's. Historically, the means of production has been collectively owned. Further, there is no distinction between members' standard of living, within a single kibbutz based on type of work. Finally, these settlements have collectivized services: dining room/kitchen facilities, children's house and laundry facilities.

2. This by no means exhausts substantive research areas of the kibbutz. Other research areas include the political-economy of the kibbutz (cf. Rayman, 1977), childcare and parent-child relations (cf. Schlesinger, 1970, whose footnotes indicate articles related to this area; Gerson, 1978), generational differences (cf. Cohen and Rosner, 1970; Blasi, 1978).

3. Unfortunately, there is little social science research on initial periods of kibbutzim. With the exception of Yonina Talmon's work, anecdotes and self-reports comprise most of the existing material. Talmon's book (1972), quoted repeatedly throughout this paper, is a series of journal articles she published in the 1950s and early 1960s.

4. Though veterans in each kibbutz, by virtue of their greater experience and seniority, did assume informal leadership, that arrangement never crystallized into a formal authority structure (cf. Hertz and Baker, 1980).

5. For a discussion of intimate relations in the kibbutz, see Baker and Hertz (1981). The family, today, is the main provider of intimacy, as they argue.

6. It remains unclear, however, how widespread sexual freedom actually was (cf. Talmon, 1972:10).

7. Talmon (1972:15) contends: "The birth of children made manifest the partial independence of the family."

8. Even where meals are consumed in private quarters, the overwhelming majority of kibbutzim purchase and prepare meals collectively. Thus, the quality or variety of food does not differ, only the location in which it is consumed.

9. An indicator of this has been a decline in the number of divorces: the rate of divorce is lower for the second generation than for the first generation (cf. Gerson, 1978:57-60; Spiro, 1979:29-30). More interesting, the communities' attitude toward divorce has changed from tolerance to a negative one (Spiro, 1979:29). Because leisure activities and holidays center around the family as a basic unit, Gerson (1979:61) contends that the divorcee feels lonely and isolated. In this regard, life for single people can be particularly difficult as well. Finally, the centrality of family in kibbutz life has created pressure on the individual to marry and/or remarry.

10. Gerson (1978:54) does report that in a few kibbutzim, World War II restitution payments from the West German government to concentration camp survivors resulted in "rich" and "poor" families. This is, however, not the case in all kibbutzim. Most recipients turned those payments over to collective projects.

11. This does not necessarily result in the creation of larger domiciles. But it results in the concentration of family members into specific and contiguous dwelling units creating neighbors based on family ties not cohort ties.

12. Rosner's findings indicate that women put family before work and social activities; men's priorities are the reverse. However, "only 27% maintained that this is desirable. It is interesting to note that the vast majority of these 27% justify their attitude by 'natural' difference between the sexes . . ." (1976:85).

13. For a comparison of sex roles in the kibbutz and in Israeli cities, see Padan-Eisenstark (1973) and Schlesinger (1977). They both argue that sex roles are more confined in the kibbutz because there are less occupational choices for women in the kibbutz than in the city.

14. It should be noted, of course, that any attempt to categorize and label different analytic approaches does violence to the sophistication of their unique arguments. This is

regrettable; however, in this limited space I will present my rationale for this categorization and as accurate a representation of the different arguments as possible.

15. It is unfortunate that researchers have chosen to focus on kibbutz members' labor only; it is critical to investigate the role of volunteer and hired labor in the kibbutz. These external labor sources may further be eroding women's employment in the productive sector.

REFERENCES

Baker, Wayne and Rosanna Hertz, "The dual opportunity structure in an Israeli kibbutz: men's and women's work." Paper presented at the Annual Meetings of the Midwest Sociological Society, Milwaukee, Wisconsin, 1980.

―――― "Communal diffusion of friendship: the structure of intimate relations in an Israeli kibbutz." In Helena Z. Lopata and David Maines (eds.), *Research in the Interweave of Social Roles,* Vol. 2. Greenwich, CT: J.A.I. Press, 1981.

Baratz, Joseph, *A Village by the Jordan.* Tel Aviv: The Department of Ichud Habonim, 1956.

Blasi, Joseph R., "Generational differences in the sense of community among kibbutz members." Paper presented at the Annual Meetings of the American Psychological Association, Toronto, Canada, 1978.

Blumberg. Rae Lesser, "From liberation to laundry: a structural interpretation of the retreat from sexual equality in the Israeli kibbutz." Paper presented at the Annual Meetings of the American Political Science Association, Chicago, Illinois, 1974.

―――― "Women and work around the world." Pp. 412-33 in A. G. Sargent (ed.), *Beyond Sex Roles,* St. Paul: West, 1977.

Bowes, Alison, "Women in the kibbutz movement." *Sociological Review* 26:237-262, 1978.

Cohen, Erik and Menachen Rosner, "Relations between generations in the Israeli kibbutz." *Journal of Contemporary History* 5:73-86, 1970.

Gerson, Menachen, "Women in the kibbutz." *American Journal of Orthopsychiatry* 41:566-573, 1971.

―――― *Family, Women and Socialization in the Kibbutz.* Reading, Mass.: D. C. Heath and Co., 1978.

Hertz, Rosanna, and Wayne Baker, "Community continuity and division: kinship in an Israeli kibbutz." Paper presented at the Annual Meetings of the Midwest Sociological Society, Milwaukee, Wisconsin, 1980.

Ichilov, Orit, and Samuel Bar, "Extended family ties and the allocation of social rewards in veteran kibbutzim in Israel." *Journal of Marriage and the Family* 42:421-426, 1980.

Keller, Suzanne, "The family in the kibbutz: what lessons for us." Pp. 115-144 in M. Curtis and M. Chertoff (eds.), *Israel: Social Structure and Change.* New Brunswick, N.J.: Transaction Books, 1973.

Mariampolski, Hyman, "Changes in kibbutz society: their implications for the situation of the sexes." *International Review of Modern Sociology* 6:201-216, 1976.

Murdock, George, *Social Structure.* New York: Macmillan, 1949.

Padan-Eisenstark, Dorit, "Are Israeli women really equal? trends and patterns of Israeli women's labor force participation: a comparative analysis." *Journal of Marriage and the Family* 35:538-545, 1973.

Rabin, A. I., "The sexes: ideology and reality in the Israeli kibbutz." Pp. 285-307 in G. H. Seward and R. C. Williamson (eds.), *Sex Roles in Changing Society.* New York: Random House, 1970.

Rayman, Paula, "Community development and nation-building: the study of an Israeli border kibbutz." Ph.D. dissertation, Department of Sociology, Boston College, 1977.

Rosner, Menachem, "Women in the kibbutz: changing status and concepts." *Asian and African Studies* 3:35-68, 1967.

———— The Kibbutz as a Way of Life in Modern Society. Givat Haviva, Israel: Center for Social Research on the Kibbutz, 1976.

Rosner, Menachem and Michael Palgi, "Family and Familism." Haifa University, Israel: Institute of Research on the Kibbutz and the Cooperative Idea, 1980.

———— "Sex Roles and Women." Haifa University, Israel: Institute of Research on the Kibbutz and the Cooperative Idea, 1980.

Schlesinger, Benjamin, "Family life in the kibbutz of Israel: utopia gained or paradise lost?" *International Journal of Comparative Sociology* 4:251-271, 1970.

Schlesinger, Yaffa, "Sex roles and social change in the kibbutz." *Journal of Marriage and the Family* 39:771-779, 1977.

Shepher, Joseph, "Familism and social structure: the case of the kibbutz." *Journal of Marriage and the Family* 31:567-583, 1969.

Spiro, Melford E., "Is the family universal?" *American Anthropologist* 56:839-846, 1954.

———— "Addendum." In Normal W. Bell and Ezra F. Vogel (eds.), *A Modern Introduction to the Family.* Glencoe: The Free Press, 1960.

———— *Kibbutz: Venture in Utopia.* New York: Schocken Press, 1963.

———— *Gender and Culture: Kibbutz women revisited.* Durham, North Carolina: Duke University Press, 1979.

Talmon, Yonina, "The family in a revolutionary movement—the case of the kibbutz in Israel." Pp. 259-286 in M. F. Nimoff (ed.), *Comparative Family Systems.* Boston: Houghton Mifflin Co., 1965.

———— *Family and Community in the kibbutz.* Cambridge: Harvard University Press, 1972.

Tiger, Lionel, and Robin Fox, *The Imperial Animal.* New York: Holt, Rinehart and Winston, 1971.

Tiger, Lionel, and Joseph Shepher, *Women in the Kibbutz.* New York: Harcourt Brace Jovanovich, 1975.

Wilson, Edward O., *Sociobiology: The New Synthesis.* Cambridge: Belknap Press of Harvard University Press, 1975.

VOLUNTARY CHILDLESSNESS IN THE 1980s:
A SIGNIFICANT INCREASE?

Sharon K. Houseknecht, PhD

Voluntary Childlessness as a Viable Option

Is voluntary childlessness a viable option for family life in the eighties? If "viable option" refers to "what is possible," then the answer is, "yes." Marriage without children was, is, and, therefore, probably will remain a viable choice. For almost two decades now, the *expected* childless rate among wives 18-39 years old has ranged from 3 to 6 percent (Table 1). Although this rate incorporates both voluntary and involuntary childlessness, recent data on reproductive impairments suggest that most of it is now voluntary. In 1976, it was estimated that only 1.5 percent of all currently married couples in the United States (with wife 15-44 years of age) were childless and non-contraceptively sterile (National Center for Health Statistics, 1980). Except in the case of sterility, where women know that it is *impossible* (not just *difficult*) for them to conceive or carry a pregnancy to term, they probably would not report on expectation to remain childless, unless, of course, their preference was to remain childless (voluntarily).

The fact that the expectation to remain permanently childless is largely deliberate at the present time means that voluntary childlessness is viewed as a viable life-style by some couples. To be viable, however, does not mean to be common and, in fact, voluntary childlessness is not.

Trends in Voluntary Childlessness

It is fascinating and perhaps surprising to some that the *expected* childless rate has changed relatively little over time. Certainly, there is not the dramatic increase that many believe has accompanied the ex-

---

Dr. Houseknecht is an Assistant Professor of Sociology at Ohio State University, Columbus, OH.

51

Table 1

Percent of Wives 18–39 Years Old Who Expect

To Remain Childless for Selected Years Between 1960 and 1978[a]

Year	All Races	White	Black
1978[b]	5.6	5.6	4.5
1977[c]	5.7	5.9	4.4
1976[d]	5.4	5.6	3.6
1975[e]	4.6	4.8	3.6
1974[e]	5.0	5.1	4.6
1973[e]	4.2	4.2	4.6
1972[e]	4.1	4.1	3.9
1971[d]	4.2	4.1	4.1
1967[d]	3.1	3.0	4.0
1960[d]	4.0	4.0	?

[a]1979 Census figures are for wives 18–34 years old and so will not be reported here with the data for 18–39 year olds.

[b]United States Bureau of the Census, 1979, Table 4.

[c]United States Bureau of Census, 1978a, Table 3.

[d]United States Bureau of Census, 1978b, Table 3–3.

[e]United States Bureau of Census, 1976b, Table 2.

pansion in educational and occupational opportunities for women in recent years. The reason for this misconception, in large part, is that only census data through 1975 and only *actual* childless rates have been used by those endeavoring to substantiate their claims (United States Bureau of the Census, 1976a; Poston and Gotard, 1977; De Jong and Sell, 1977; Mattessich, 1979). An examination of the most recent census data suggests that, although viable, voluntarily childless marriages are not likely to become any more common in the 1980s.

Table 2 presents the percent of ever-married white women who are *actually* childless by age for selected years between 1940 and 1979. It is clear that actual childless rates have varied considerably over time. From 1940 to 1960, there was a persistent *decline* for all age groups which was probably due in large part to reductions in involuntary childlessness as a result of advances in nutrition and medicine (Glick, 1977). Looking just

Table 2

Percent of Ever-Married White Women Who are Actually Childless

By Age for Selected Years Between 1940 and 1979

Age Categories	Year									
	1940[a]	1950[b]	1960[c]	1965[d]	1970[e]	1975[f]	1976[g]	1977[h]	1978[i]	1979[j]
20-24	36.9	34.0	25.0	28.7	37.7	45.1	44.2	44.4	43.0	42.4
25-29	27.2	20.1	12.3	11.8	16.1	21.7	22.4	25.5	26.3	27.4
30-34	20.6	15.8	9.7	7.0	8.1	9.0	10.8	11.6	11.8	13.4
35-39	17.1	17.5	10.2	8.1	7.0	5.3	6.4	6.9	7.0	7.1

[a]United States Bureau of the Census, 1943, Table 1.

[b]United States Bureau of Census, 1955, Table 2.

[c]United States Bureau of Census, 1976a, Table 6.

[d]United States Bureau of Census, 1969, Table 1.

[e]United States Bureau of the Census, 1976a, Table 6.

[f]United States Bureau of the Census, 1976a, Table 6.

[g]United States Bureau of the Census, 1977a, Table 4.

[h]United States Bureau of the Census, 1978a, Table 6.

[i]United States Bureau of the Census, 1979a, Table 4.

[j]United States Bureau of the Census, 1980a, Table 4.

at the 20-24 age category, we see that there was a steady *increase* from 1960 until 1975. However, starting with 1976 and continuing each year through 1979 (except for one very minor exception), the rate consistently declined. The proportion of white women who were in the 20-24 age category and childless went from 45.1 in 1975 to 42.4 in 1979. More important than this 2.7 percentage point decrease is the consistently declining pattern over the five-year period which may indicate the beginning of a downward trend.

Thus far, this downward prediction is based only on the experience of the 20-24 age group. However, in the analysis of fertility, this category is the most important one because it is these women that have most of their reproductive lifespan ahead of them (United States Bureau of the Census, 1978b). A decrease in the actual childless rate has implications for voluntary childlessness because it suggests that the postponement of childbearing phenomenon that became prevalent in the early seventies (Gibson, 1976) may be subsiding. Postponement is directly related to the childless decision since the majority of voluntarily childless wives do not decide at a relatively early age in life, before marriage, to remain childless. Rather, they make their decision after they have developed a lifestyle that they do not want to give up (Veevers, 1973; Bram, 1974; McLaughlin, et al., 1974; Marcks, 1976; Nason and Poloma, 1977; Houseknecht, 1979a; 1979c). Therefore, a reduction in postponement would mean that fewer women would have sufficient time for the childless decision to evolve.

It was earlier noted that "actual" childlessness includes women who are intending to have children at some future time as well as those who are either voluntarily or involuntarily childless. That the continuing decrease in actual childlessness within the 20-24 age group is largely due to the postponement component is supported by the fact that the proportion of *childless wives* (as opposed to all wives) who considered themselves to be postponers declined between 1976 and 1978 (United States Bureau of the Census, 1977b; 1979b). This decrease can be linked to a trend in society at large: Many believe that young people specifically and the society generally have changed in recent years so that there is now a greater inclination to be traditional, conservative, and family oriented. The anti-ERA, anti-abortion and traditional family movements are all part of the change. This assessment fits with the finding that more young women are having children earlier in life.

It might be argued that predicting voluntary childless rates on the basis of 20-24 year old *ever-married* women is misleading. After all, growing

Table 3

Actual and Expected Childless Rates for 20-24 Year

Old White Women[a] for Selected Years and Marital Statuses

Year	Single Women		All Women	
	Actual	Expected	Actual	Expected
1979[b]	93.8	18.3	66.5	11.8
1978[c]	94.2	19.5	66.1	11.9
1977	95.7[b]	18.6[d]	66.6[b]	11.8[d]
1976	95.3[c]	19.2[e]	65.2[c]	10.5[e]

[a]The only exception in this regard are the actual rates for all women and they apply to all races.

[b]United States Bureau of the Census, 1980b, Tables 5, 6, 7.

[c]United States Bureau of the Census, 1979b, Tables 4, 5, 6, 8.

[d]United States Bureau of the Census, 1978a, Tables 3, 4.

[e]United States Bureau of the Census, 1977b, Tables 4, 14.

numbers of women are postponing marriage beyond this age category and for them childlessness may be increasing at a phenomenal rate. To rule out this possibility, data for 20-24 year old never-married white women are examined for the period 1976-1979 in Table 3. These women do not experience a phenomenal increase but rather by a small decline in *actual* childlessness. The most important question is whether increasing proportions of 20-24 year old single women expect to remain childless after they are married. The figures presented in Table 3 suggest that this is *not* the case for the time period under consideration.

The 1976-1979 decline in the percent childless for 20-24 year old single and ever-married women is not observed when both marital categories are combined (Table 3). This seeming anomaly is due to the fact that single women are becoming a bigger part of the whole and they have higher rates of childlessness than ever-married women.

It is true that the data presented in Table 2 evidence a continuing *in-*

crease in *actual* childlessness for the 25-29, 30-34, and 35-39 age groups. However, we can see also that the increase in childlessness that first began between 1960 and 1965 for the 20-24 age group only gradually spread to the older age categories at about five year intervals. This means, of course, that it was the same people for the most part who were responsible for the initial change in each age group.

Even though the increase in *actual* childlessness continues for the older age categories, there has recently been a leveling off in the proportions of wives who *expect* to remain childless. In fact, Table 4 shows that this was the case for both the 20-24 and 25-29 age categories between 1977 and 1979. Women 30-34 years old are the only exception. This latter finding does not negate the argument, however, since a *short-term* increase in the phenomenon in the older age categories is to be expected given the importance of the postponement factor in the decision to remain voluntarily childless.

In conclusion, the *long-term* trend in the voluntary childless rate appears to be downward, or at least not upward. To suggest that there will not be a significant increase in childlessness in the United States is to take a rather controversial stance since it disputes the commonly held notion

Table 4

Percent of White Wives Who Expect No Lifetime Births

By Age: 1975 to 1979

Age Categories	Year				
	1975[a]	1976[b]	1977[c]	1978[d]	1979[e]
20–24	4.7	4.3	5.7	5.5	5.7
25–29	4.9	6.7	6.6	5.9	5.5
30–34	5.5	5.8	6.1	5.4	6.4

[a]United States Bureau of the Census, 1976b, Table H.

[b]United States Bureau of the Census, 1977b, Table 12.

[c]United States Bureau of the Census, 1978a, Table 3.

[d]United States Bureau of the Census, 1979b, Table 4.

[e]United States Bureau of the Census, 1980b, Table 5.

that the phenomenon will continue to become more widespread (Bumpass, 1973; Grindstaff, 1976; DeJong and Sell, 1977; Poston and Gotard, 1977; Westoff, 1978; Marciano, 1978; Veevers, 1979). However, based on this analysis of the most recent census data, it does seem unlikely that voluntary childlessness will soon reach Veevers' (1979:7) predicted rate of "at least 10 percent."

No Significant Increase—Why Not?

It is the combination of choice and permanence that serve to distinguish deliberate childlessness from that which is due to impaired fecundity, delayed childbearing, or uncertainty. When *voluntary* childlessness is defined in this way, it is clear that the increase that was predicted on the basis of demographic variables, i.e., female education and employment, has not happened. The pervasive normative change regarding childbearing that was expected to accompany career opportunities for women did not occur. Voluntary childlessness is still considered deviant.

In 1976, Ory found that "When differences were perceived, parents tended, in most cases, to characterize childless couples in terms of the undesirable meanings of nonparenthood, such as more selfish, less religious, less responsible, less happily married, less mature, less natural, less feminine or masculine and for females, more likely to have mental problems." Selfishness was the modal response. In 1978, Polit looked at family size effects and reported that "the voluntarily childless person was perceived as less socially desirable, less well adjusted, less nurturant, more autonomous, more succorant, and more socially distant than individuals of other fertility statuses."

Jamison et al. (1979) considered attitudes toward women and men separately. His results show that the child free woman was rated as more selfish, less happy, less well-adjusted emotionally, less likely to get along with her parents, significantly less sensitive and loving, and less likely to be happy and satisfied at age 65 than mothers. Similarly, the child free husband was seen as significantly less well-adjusted emotionally, less sensitive and loving, and as having a less fulfilling life than the otherwise identical father of two. In 1979, Blake published data on attitudes toward childlessness which had been obtained through a 1977 Gallup survey of voting-age adults in the United States. She concluded that, "Despite the claims of the nonparenthood literature, the childless are not seen as enjoying the most satisfying lifestyle, nor are they seen as having the most satisfying marriages." In 1980 Calhoun and Selby found that, "The husband with children was perceived as less disturbed than either the voluntarily or involuntarily childless husband."

That there is very limited support for encouraging people to consider options and make a choice with regard to parenthood was further demonstrated June 27, 1979, on QUBE T.V. in Columbus, Ohio, an experimental system in which the viewing audience can make instant responses to posed questions. A shocking 69% would not approve of classroom discussions that included even mention of nonparenthood as a possible lifestyle choice.

It seems clear after reviewing the stereotype findings that the voluntarily childless are still not considered "normal" but rather are imputed to have a number of undesirable attributes. Stereotyping of couples with no children is more negative than stereotyping of couples with more than four children (Ory, 1976). In fact, Hoffman (ISR Newsletter, 1978) found that 58 percent of both mothers and fathers would choose to have six children rather than none at all.

The very high value that is placed on having children by all sectors of this society has implications for socialization, which, of course, involves internalization of expectations. This means that many women have children without considering the possibility of not having them. Others may prefer a childless lifestyle but still have children because of the strong pressures and sanctions that they encounter.[1] Although career women have smaller families, a preponderance of two children rather than three or four (U.S. Bureau of the Census, 1980a), two, three or four children families are variations which fall within the *acceptable* normative fertility range of the society.

It appears, then, that career opportunities alone are not sufficient but must be accompanied by social support if a woman is, in fact, to remain childless. Some evidence for these ideas is available. In two separate studies (Houseknecht, 1977a; 1978a), the existence and extent of reference group support for a childless life-style was found to be significantly greater for voluntarily childless respondents than for future/current parents. Certainly, such reference-other support would help alleviate the effects of pressures and sanctions levied by dissenting groups and individuals.

In conclusion, both career involvement and reference group support have been found to be significant factors in the decision to remain childless. Together, they help to make voluntary childlessness a viable lifestyle option. Both are important but both are not increasing. We have seen that societal tolerance is not widespread. Until this situation changes, expanding female achievement opportunities are not likely to substantially promote voluntary childlessness or even the one-child family.

Voluntary Childlessness and Gender Equality

Although it cannot be said that most career-oriented women want to remain childless, most voluntarily childless women are, in fact, career-oriented. Previous research has shown that a strong determinant of aspiration among women is an egalitarian sex role ideology (Lipman-Blumen, 1972). This same variable also has been found to be inversely associated with both the number of children women intend to have and the number they actually do have (Scanzoni, 1975). Therefore, it might be expected that voluntarily childless couples would more strongly endorse egalitarian gender role norms than couples at large (Reiss, 1980). Even though a notable increase in voluntary childlessness is not forecasted for the 1980s, it is still important to discuss the significance of this life-style to gender equality in marital relationships given its current emphasis.

Voluntarily childless women tend to have a less traditional view of the female role than other women. This has been demonstrated in many studies (Bram, 1974; Welds, 1977; Hamilton, 1977; Toomey, 1977; den Bandt, 1980; Houseknecht, 1978b; Polonko, 1978; Teicholz, 1978; Fisher, 1979; Houseknecht, 1979b; Hoffman and Levant, 1980). In only two instances in which women were considered separately are these findings not supported (Ory, 1976; Levine, 1978). Not surprisingly, comparative research also indicates that voluntarily childless women have a greater identification with the Women's Movement (Bram, 1974; Toomey, 1977; Houseknecht, 1978b; Chalfant, 1979).

When *males* and *couples* are the units of analysis, the association between childbearing intentions and sex role ideology is less clear cut. Bram (1974) and Fisher (1979) reported that their voluntarily childless males had less stereotypic sex role attitudes than other males but Brown and Magarick (1978) and Hoffman and Levant (1980) found no difference. Focusing on *couples,* Burnside (1977) and Silka and Keisler (1977) also reported no difference.

Role Sharing

The financial role. To what extent is ideological commitment to equality translated into role sharing? For one thing, voluntarily childless women have a greater share of the financial role in marriage than women in general. Most comparative studies have found that women who choose never to have children are more likely to participate in the labor force (Bram, 1974; Ory, 1976; Brown and Magarick, 1978; Polonko, 1978; Dietz, 1979; Scott, 1979). Some indication as to how high labor force participation rates actually are is provided by several descriptive studies. In all of the samples, approximately 90 percent or more of the childless women were employed outside the home (Holz, 1975; Veevers, 1975; Thoen, 1977; Marciano, 1978; Baum and Cope, 1979; Hall, 1979).

There is extensive evidence that the earnings of voluntarily childless women are far above average (Gustavus and Henley, 1971; McLaughlin, *et al.*, 1974; Hotz, 1975; Burnside, 1977; Goodbody, 1977; Polonko, 1978; Dietz, 1979; Houseknecht, 1979c). Interestingly, there is some indication that the income situation for voluntarily childless females may not hold for voluntarily childless males. Dietz (1979), for example, using data from the 1965 National Fertility Survey, found that the husband's income is inversely related to voluntary childlessness, i.e., the higher the husband's income, the more likely a couple will intend a first birth. Burnside (1977) also reported that parent husbands in the sample earned higher median incomes than voluntarily childless husbands.

In sum, women who choose never to have children are more likely than other women to participate in the labor force, and, second, they tend to earn higher than average incomes. The fact that voluntarily childless families seem to earn incomes that are more or less equivalent to those of parent families, even with these two apparent advantages, is further evidence that the childless male's contribution to family income is proportionately lower than average. Thus, although the voluntarily childless male tends to be employed in a high status position (Gustavus and Henley, 1971; Silka and Keisler, 1977; Brown and Magarick, 1978; Baum and Cope, 1979; Hoffman and Levant, 1980), his job does not seem to provide remuneration that is comparable to its status. On the other hand, the data indicate that the voluntarily childless woman is contributing a larger proportion to the family income than is the employed mother. Although further evidence is needed on this issue, these findings suggest that the voluntarily childless may have a more egalitarian spousal relationship. The reduction in economic and psychological dependency that is usually associated with female career commitment serves to further support this notion.

The housekeeper role. Since voluntarily childless wives typically share a major part of the financial role in marriage, it is relevant to consider to what extent their husbands engage in domestic task sharing. In this connection, Houseknecht (1979b) found that voluntarily childless women reported greater spousal agreement on household tasks than did mothers. This finding, of course, does not reveal who was doing what. It only indicates that the childless women were more satisfied with the ways in which these matters were being handled in their marriage. However, a recent longitudinal study concluded that education and employment are the most important variables for predicting women's gender role attitudes (Mason et al., 1976). It was found that well-educated women and those with the most recent employment experiences held more egalitarian attitudes. Voluntarily childless women in comparative studies have been characterized by unusually high levels of education (Bram, 1974; McLaughlin, et al., 1974; Burnside, 1977; Toomey, 1977; Brown and Magarick, 1978; Houseknecht, 1978a) and, as was previously noted, labor force participation (Bram, 1974; Ory, 1976; Brown and Magarick, 1978; Polonko, 1978; Dietz, 1979; Scott, 1979). Therefore, it seems probable that the greater extent of interspousal agreement on household tasks reported by childless women implies that their husbands were more inclined to share the housekeeper role. Bram (1974), in fact, found that voluntarily childless couples were more nearly equal in their division of household labor than were parents or postponers (as reported by both wives and husbands).

The decision making role. In terms of decisions that have a joint effect on the couple, Bram (1974) reported that childless women scored higher on joint decisions than did parents or postponers. Even in joint decisions, however, there is usually an initiator and so it seems pertinent to ask, "Who is responsible for initiating childlessness?" The available data suggest that women generally are the first to consider not having children (Burnside, 1977; Houseknecht, 1977b; Bram, 1974; Nason and Poloma, 1976; Ory, 1976; Silka and Keisler, 1977). Career development, which includes higher levels of education, enhances the likelihood that a woman will consider a childless life style. It also promotes a higher level of communication between her and her husband (Hollenbach, 1980) which enables her to convey her preferences to him.

Exactly how a wife might persuade her spouse to forego the parenting role is unclear. Quite possibly, it is through the use of "legitimate" power, or authority. According to Raven et al. (1975), this type of power is based on the acceptance of a particular role structure giving the other person the right to request compliance and giving one the duty to comply. Parenthood is generally recognized as the primary role for women but not for men in this society, probably because the major responsibility for childcare is assumed by women which means that their lives are more affected. In fact, research supports the idea that males are less ego-involved in the issue of fertility than females (Houseknecht, 1974; Harrell, et al., 1976; Lichtman, 1976; Silka and Keisler, 1977). In this connection, decision making has been found to vary by specific area and to reflect the specific interests, involvement, and time constraints of the individuals involved (Morelock, 1976, Douglas and Wind, 1978). This being the case, it is understandable how the wife's preference might carry more weight than the husband's in the final fertility decision.

Summary

The overall evidence suggests that voluntarily childless couples do have a high degree of gender equality in their marital relationships, in fact, higher than that of couples with children. This conclusion calls into question Blake and del Pinal's (1981) recent statement " . . . that an increase in nonparenthood may be checked by greater egalitarianism between marital partners . . ." Their prediction is based on a study of voting-age adults in the United States in which they examined respondents' perceptions of children as involving direct and indirect costs, financial and social investments. They found that sex role attitudes had a dramatic effect in explaining variability among respondents and concluded that "egalitarianism would help to mitigate the one strike that reproduction seems to have against it—a perception that it entails heavy *direct* costs, particularly for women" (emphasis mine).

This argument is intriguing, but there are two methodological problems associated with it. First, there is a pronatalist assumption that the voluntarily childless *would really like to have children* but sacrifice doing so in order to achieve other goals that would be difficult to attain with the conventionally-structured sex roles that accompany child rearing. Actually, there is no evidence to date that the voluntarily childless view the absence of children as a trade off. Rather, they associate very few advantages with parenthood (Houseknecht, 1978b).

A second complication in Blake and del Pinal's (1981) argument has to do with extrapolating from the general population to a special population, i.e., the voluntarily childless. They use a linear model which implies that higher egalitarianism is associated with lower costs and higher benefits of children. This model unfortunately, doesn't work below parity sizes of one. Zero always has special characteristics, mathematically and otherwise. In the case of the voluntarily childless, higher egalitarianism is associated with the perception of higher costs and lower benefits of children, not lower costs and higher benefits. This point is clear in that the voluntarily childless (unlike the respondents in Blake and del Pinal's study) recognize *indirect* costs of parenthood. In fact, two of the stated motives for remaining childless are synonymous with what Blake and del Pinal consider *indirect* costs: (1) desire for greater couple intimacy—"a more satisfactory relationship" is a statement of motive for the childless lifestyle that appears with the second highest frequency across studies; (2) job chances—"female career considerations" is a statement of motive for the childless lifestyle that appears with the third highest frequency across studies.

In sum, the trend in the rate of voluntary childlessness in the 1980s will be if not downward at least not upward. However, this prediction does not rest on the notion of greater egalitarianism between marital partners. The evidence reviewed indicates that the correlation between egalitarianism and voluntary childlessness is positive, not negative. The expected no increase in the incidence of childlessness is based on the recent changes in society towards less social approval for childlessness. The trend is towards child blessed families and traditional, conservative family values.

Voluntary Childlessness and Social Policy

"What is the significance of voluntary childlessness for society generally?" The answer to this question has implications for the successful implementation of any social policy designed to enhance the social status of individuals choosing this lifestyle.

The United States is a pronatalist society, i.e., it encourages reproduction. The norm is to have more than one child, the only child family is viewed to be incomplete. The acceptable family size range is two to four children (Family Planning Perspectives, 1977). Individuals are socialized from the beginning to this norm, and most eventually internalize it and believe it is *right*. Few people consider the possibility of not having children. This is evidence of successful socialization. It is rather a matter of deciding *when* and *how many*. Given this social context, it is understandable that to encounter someone who has *chosen* not to have children might be an uncomfortable experience because it increases awareness of childbearing options.

Research has demonstrated that the problems faced by the voluntarily childless stem from strong normative prescriptions and not from problematic personalities. Still, we have seen that the negative stereotypes continue to persist. This finding is not surprising since it is through the use of positive and negative sanctions that norms are enforced. By rewarding parents and penalizing nonparents, society increases the probability that people will have children.

There is very little support for mitigating the problems that voluntarily childless couples face because it is believed that an increase in childlessness would be damaging to society as a whole. Social policies express intentions. They are designed to produce a change from current status toward some preferred state, or to prevent movement toward a less preferred state. The "preferred" state now exists currently. As was noted earlier, the proportion of people who choose this lifestyle is very low, and there is no notable increase forecasted for the 1980s.

Since social policies reflect goals and priorities, some will argue that the goal is *not* to increase the proportion of voluntarily childless individuals. Rather it is to reduce the stigma and discrimination experienced by those who do make this choice. The counter argument is, of course, that to do so would probably have the former effect as well and so it remains an undesirable change. As long as the goal of policy formulation and program planning is to help the "individual," not "society," society is reluctant to respond. This lack of response is especially likely when the numbers advocating change are small and there is lack of organized protest. It is true that there is an organization supporting reproductive choice that was formed in 1971—The National Alliance for Optional Parenthood. However, one pressure group dedicated to legal and other specific social reforms does not constitute a social movement, and, in fact, only a small proportion of the voluntarily childless belong to this organization. Social movements arise when a social problem becomes so widespread and intense that large numbers of people are personally and deeply affected by it to the extent that they join efforts (Sherif, 1976). Certainly this situation does not exist with voluntary childlessness.

Actually, the potential gains from a reduction in pronatalism would extend beyond the childless themselves—to other adults and children as well. Although very important, this fact is not widely recognized. Those who have children without considering the possibility of not having them do not make a *decision* on what is best for their life style preference. In parenting, one frequently has to give up some of his/her creativity and self-development, and this sacrifice could result in resentment if there is an extremely strong commitment to some other sphere of life. An awareness of requisite accommodations has profound implications for effective parenting. To minimize any resentment that might arise in connection with parental obligations, such concessions must be freely chosen.

In addition to problems created by people not making a decision with regard to childbearing, there are also difficulties for people making a decision but who do not feel free to carry it out. To prefer a childless lifestyle but to succumb to societal pressures, for whatever reason, has negative implications for the well-being of children as well as the parents. This point is demonstrated in a nine-year study that compared children born to women twice denied abortions with children born to mothers who had not applied for abortion (Dytrych et al., 1975). The results indicated that the unwanted children were likely to suffer illness, problems with school, engaged in deviant behaviors and have low social acceptance than other children with similar backgrounds and inheritance.

The concept of unwantedness is problematic not only for the parents and children involved but also for society at large. Everyone shares the responsibility for neglected and abused children, at least financially, if not psychologically. Everyone loses when such children do not become productive members of the society in which they live. Unfortunately, the major emphasis of child advocacy programs has been to improve the situation of children *after they are born*. There has not been an equivalent attempt to encourage postponement of parenthood and responsible fertility decision making.

In summary, there is a real need to develop and implement a social policy whose goal is to increase choice awareness and to enhance freedom to choose. As we have seen, responsible decision making in the reproductive sphere would have positive implications for (1) the voluntarily childless; (2) adults with unwanted children; (3) unwanted children; and (4) society at large.

NOTES

1. There is ample evidence that the United States is a pronatalist society (for example, Blake, 1972; Griffith, 1973; Houseknecht, forthcoming).

REFERENCE LIST

Baum, Frances and David R. Cope, "Some characteristics of intentionally childless wives in Britain." *Journal of Biosocial Science* 12:287-299, 1980.

Blake, Judith, "Coercive pronatalism and American population policy." Research paper prepared for the Commission on Population and The American Future, University of California International Population and Urban Research, Berkeley, 1972.

Blake, Judith, "Is zero preferred? American attitudes toward childlessness in the 1970's." *Journal of Marriage and the Family* 41:245-257, 1979.

Blake, Judith and Jorge H. del Pinal, "The childlessness option: recent American views of nonparenthood." In Gerry E. Hendershot and Paul J. Placek (Eds.), *Predicting Fertility*. Lexington, Massachusetts: Lexington Books, 1981.

Bram, Susan, "To have or have not: A social psychological study of voluntarily childless couples, parents-to-be, and parents." Unpublished Ph.D. Dissertation, University of Michigan, 1974.

Brown, Robert A. and Ronald H. Margarick, "Social and emotional aspects of voluntary childlessness in vasectomized childless men." Paper presented at the annual meeting of the American Psychological Association, Toronto, Ontario, 1978.

Bumpass, Larry L., "Is low fertility here to stay?" *Family Planning Perspectives* 5:67-69, 1973.

Burnside, Beverly, "Gender roles and lifestyles: A socioculture study of voluntary childlessness." Unpublished Ph.D. Dissertation, University of Washington, 1977.

Calhoun, Lawrence and James W. Selby, "Voluntary childlessness, involuntary childlessness, and having children: A study of social perceptions." *Family Relations* 29:181-183, 1980.

Chalfant, H. Paul, "Childlessness: A multivariate profile of a national sample." Unpublished manuscript, Texas Tech University, 1979.

DeJong, G. F. and R. R. Sell, "Changes in childlessness in the United States: A demographic path and analysis." *Population Studies* 31:129-141, 1977.

den Bandt, Marie-Louise, "Voluntary childlessness in the Netherlands." *Alternative Lifestyles* 3:329-349, 1980.

Dietz, Thomas, "Factors influencing childlessness among American women." Unpublished Ph.D. Dissertation, University of California, Davis, California, 1979.

Douglas, S. P. and Y. Wind, "Examining family role and authority patterns; Two methodological issues." *Journal of Marriage and the Family* 40:35-47, 1978.

Dytrych, Zdenek, Zdenek Matejcek, Vratislav Schaller, Henry P. David, Herbert L. Friedman, "Children born to women denied abortion." *Family Planning Perspectives* 7:165-171, 1975.

———— "U. S. wives 18-24 expect 2.1 children; singles 1.9" *Family Planning Perspectives* 3:133-134, 1977.

Fisher, Pamila J., "Optional parenthood: Do young adults really have a choice?" *Optional Parenthood Today* 7:7, 1979.

Gibson, Campbell, "The U. S. fertility decline, 1961-1975: The contribution of changes in marital status and marital fertility." *Family Planning Perspectives* 8:249-252, 1976.

Glick, Paul, "Updating the life cycle of the family." *Journal of Marriage and the Family* 39:5-13, 1977.

Goodbody, Sandra Toll, "Psychosocial implications of voluntary childlessness." *Social Casework* 58:426-434, 1977.

Griffith, Janet, "Social pressure on family size intentions." *Family Planning Perspectives* 5:237-242, 1973.

Grindstaff, Carl F., "Trends and incidence of childlessness by race: Indicators of black progress over three decades." *Sociological Focus* 9:265-284, 1976.

Gustavus, Susan O. and James R. Henley Jr., "Correlates of voluntary childlessness in a select population." *Social Biology* 18:277-284, 1971.

Hall, Dorothy Davis, "Coping behaviors of voluntarily childless wives." Unpublished masters thesis, The Ohio State University, 1979.

Hamilton, Mary Ruth, "Application of utility-cost decision model to a comparison of intentionally childless couples and parent couples." Ph.D. Dissertation, University of Maryland. Dissertation Abstracts International 38:2360-A, 1977.

Harrell, Jan E., Nancy McCunney, and Beverly Kithcart, "Explaining fertility behavior:

Sex roles and the couple relationship from the male's perspective." Paper presented at the annual meeting of the National Council on Family Relations, New York, 1976.

Hoffman, Susan R. and Ronald F. Levant, "A comparison of childfree and child-anticipated married couples in relation to marital and psychological variables." Unpublished manuscript, Northeastern University, 1980.

Hollenbach, Paula E., "Power in families, communication and fertility decision-making." Center for Policy Studies Working Paper 53. New York, New York: The Population Council, 1980.

Hotz, Joyce Novel, "An investigation of the nature and defense of voluntary childlessness." Unpublished manuscript, Douglass College, 1975.

Houseknecht, Sharon K., "Social psychological aspects of voluntary childlessness." Unpublished masters thesis, Pennsylvania State University, 1974.

Houseknecht, Sharon K., "Reference group support for voluntary childlessness: Evidence for conformity." *Journal of Marriage and the Family* 39:285-292, 1977a.

Housekneet, Sharon K., "Wives but not mothers: Factors influencing the decision to remain childless." Unpublished Ph.D. Dissertation, Pennsylvania State University, 1977b.

Housekneet, Sharon K., "Achieving females and the decision to remain childless: A missing link." Paper presented at the annual meeting of the Groves Conference on Marriage and Family, Washington, D. C., 1978a.

Houseknecht, Sharon K., "A social psychological model of voluntary childlessness." *Alternative Lifestyles* 1:379-402, 1978b.

Houseknecht, Sharon K., "Timing of the decision to remain voluntarily childless: Evidence for continuous socialization." *Psychology of Women Quarterly* 4:81-96, 1979a.

Houseknecht, Sharon K., "Childlessness and marital adjustment." *Journal of Marriage and the Family* 41:259-265, 1979b.

Houseknecht, Sharon K., "Female employment and reduced family size: Some insight on the direction of the relationship." Paper presented at the annual meeting of the American Sociological Association, Boston, 1979c.

Houseknecht, Sharon K., "Voluntary childlessness: A critical review." In Marvin B. Sussman and Suzanne K. Steinmetz (Eds.), *Handbook of Marriage and the Family*. New York, New York: Plenum, forthcoming.

ISR Newletter, "Why couples choose parenthood." Institute for Social Research, The University of Michigan, 1978.

Jamison, Pollyann H., Louis R. Franzini, Robert M. Kaplan, "Some assumed characteristics of voluntarily childfree women and men." Psychology of Women Quarterly 4:266-273, 1979.

Levine, Janice Oppenheim, "Voluntarily childfree women and mothers: A comparative study." Unpublished Ph.D. Dissertation, Michigan State University, 1978.

Lichtman, Carl Herbert, "'Voluntary' childlessness: A thematic analysis of the person and the process." Ph.D. Dissertation, Columbia University Teacher's College, Dissertation Abstracts International 37:1484-85, 1976.

Lipman-Blumen, Jean, "How ideology shapes women's lives." *Scientific American* 226:34-42, 1972.

McLaughlin, Marcia, Katherine Rohrer, and Beverly Toomey, "Exploratory study of childless women choosing sterilization as the contraceptive method." Unpublished manuscript, The Ohio State University, 1974.

Marciano, Teresa Donati, "Male pressure in the decision to remain childfree." *Alternative Lifestyles* 1:95-112, 1978.

Marcks, Beatrice Raynor, "Voluntarily childless couples: An explanatory study." Unpublished masters thesis, Syracuse University, 1976.

Mason, Karen Oppenheim, John L. Czajka, Sara Arber, "Change in U. S. women's sex-role attitudes, 1964-1974." *American Sociological Review* 41:573-596, 1976.

Mattessich, Paul W., "Childlessness and its correlates in historical perspective: A research note." *Journal of Family History* 4:299-307, 1979.

Morelock, Judy C., "Sex differences in compliance." Paper presented at the annual meeting of the Midwest Sociological Society, St. Louis, Missouri, 1976.

Nason, Ellen Mara and Margaret M. Poloma, *Voluntary Childless Couples: The Emergence of a Variant Lifestyle*. Beverly Hills, California: Sage Publications, 1977.

Ory, Marcia, "The decision to parent or not: Normative and structural components." Unpublished Ph.D. Dissertation, Purdue University, 1976.

Polit, Denise F., "Stereotypes relating to family size status." *Journal of Marriage and the Family* 40:105-116, 1978.

Polonko, Karen, "A comparison of the patterns associated with voluntary childlessness and low birth intentions." Paper presented at the annual meeting of the American Sociological Association, San Francisco, 1978.

Poston, Dudley L., Jr., and Erin Gotard, "Trends in childlessness in the United States, 1910-1975." *Social Biology* 24:212-224, 1977.

Raven, B. J., R. Centers and A. Rodrigues, "The bases of conjugal power." In R. E. Cromwell and D. H. Olson (Eds.), *Power in Families*. New York, New York: Sage Publications, 1975.

Reiss, Ira L., *Family Systems in America* (3rd Edition). New York: Holt, Reinhart and Winston, 1980.

Scanzoni, John, *Sex Roles, Life Styles, and Childbearing: Changing Patterns in Marriage and the Family*. New York, New York: Free Press, 1975.

Scott, Lucy, "Intentionally childless women: An exploration of psychosocial and psychosexual factors." Unpublished manuscript, The Fielding Institute, 1979.

Sherif, Carolyn Wood, *Orientation In Social Psychology*. New York, New York: Harper and Row, 1976.

Silka, Linda and Sara Kiesler, "Couples who choose to remain childless." *Family Planning Perspectives* 9:16-25, 1977.

Teicholz, Judith Guss, "Psychological correlates of voluntary childlessness in married women." Paper presented at the annual meeting of the Eastern Psychological Association, Washington, D.C., 1978.

Thoen, Gail Ann, "Commitment among voluntary childfree couples to a variant lifestyle." Unpublished Ph.D. Dissertation, University of Minnesota, 1977.

Toomey, Beverly Guella, "College women and voluntary childlessness: A comparative study of women indicating they want to have children and those indicating they do not want to have children." Unpublished Ph.D. Dissertation, The Ohio State University, 1977.

U. S. Bureau of the Census, *United States census of the population: 1940*. Washington, D.C.: U. S. Government Printing Office, 1943.

U. S. Bureau of the Census, *United States census of the population: 1950*. Washington, D.C.: U. S. Government Printing Office, 1955.

U. S. Bureau of the Census, *Marriage, Fertility and Childspacing: June 1965*. Current Population Reports. Series P-20, No. 186. Washington, D.C.: U. S. Government Printing Office, 1969.

U. S. Bureau of the Census, *Fertility and the Prospects of American Women: June 1975*. Current Population Reports. Series P-20, No. 288. Washington, D.C.: U. S. Government Printing Office, 1976a.

U. S. Bureau of the Census, *Fertility of American Women: June 1975*. Current Population Reports. Series P-20, No. 301. Washington, D.C.: U. S. Government Printing Office, 1976b.

U. S. Bureau of the Census, *Population Profile of the United States: 1976*. Current Population Reports. Series P-20, No. 37. Washington, D.C.: U. S. Government Printing Office, 1977a.

U. S. Bureau of the Census. *Fertility of American Women: June 1976.* Current Population Reports. Series P-20, No. 308. Washington, D.C.: U. S. Government Printing Office, 1977b.

U. S. Bureau of the Census, *Fertility of American Women: June 1977.* Current Population Reports. Series P-20, No. 325. Washington, D.C.: U. S. Government Printing Office, 1978a.

U. S. Bureau of the Census, *Perspectives on American Fertility.* Current Population Reports. Series P-23, No. 70. Washington, D.C.: U. S. Government Printing Office, 1978b.

U. S. Bureau of the Census, *Population Profile of the United States.* Current Population Reports. Series P-20, No. 336. Washington, D.C.: U. S. Government Printing Office, 1979a.

U. S. Bureau of the Census, *Fertility of American Women: June 1978.* Current Population Reports. Series P-20, No. 341. Washington, D.C.: U. S. Government Printing Office, 1979b.

U. S. Bureau of the Census, *Population Profile of the United States: 1979.* Current Population Reports. Series P-20, No. 350. Washington, D.C.: U. S. Government Printing Office, 1980a.

U. S. Bureau of the Census, *Fertility of American Women: June 1979.* Current Population Reports. Series P-20, No. 358. Washington, D.C.: U. S. Government Printing Office, 1980b.

U. S. National Center for Health Statistics, *Reproductive Impairment Among Currently Married Couples: United States, 1976.* Advance Data, No. 55. Washington, D.C.: U. S. Government Printing Office, 1980c.

Veevers, J. E., "Voluntary childless wives: An exploratory study." *Sociology and Social Research* 57:356-366, 1973.

Veevers, J. E., "The life style of voluntarily childless couples." In Lyle Larson (Ed.), *The Canadian Family in Comparative Perspective.* Toronto, Canada: Prentice-Hall, 1975.

Veevers, J. E., "Voluntary childlessness: A review of issues and evidence." *Marriage and Family Review* 2: pp. 1:3-26, 1979.

Welds, Kathryn, "Voluntary childlessness in professional women." Paper presented at the annual meeting of the American Psychological Association, San Francisco, 1977.

Westoff, Charles F., "Some speculations on the future of marriage and fertility." *Family Planning Perspectives* 10:79-83, 1978.

COMMUTER MARRIAGES:
A REVIEW

Naomi Gerstel, PhD
Harriet Engel Gross, PhD

Introduction

The passing of a decade invariably prompts efforts to determine the essence of the period's impact on our lives, as if intrinsic meaning inheres in decennial units. The seventies, we are told, produced "The Self" earning for this effort epithets such as the "Me" and the "Narcissistic" decade (Turner, 1976; Wolf, 1976; Lasch, 1979). Along with cultural permission to cultivate our psyches went an interest in, and tolerance for, variety in the ways people went about combining commitment to the two basic arenas of modern life: work and family. The term "alternative lifestyles" entered common parlance (was even used in the title of a scholarly journal launched in mid-decade), evoking images of all manner of possibilities for extending marital and work roles beyond their previous conventional boundaries. One such alternative—marriages of professional spouses who maintain separate residences in the service of dual-careers—became predictably more noticeable as the decade wore on. First journalists and then social scientists acknowledged the effect career/family conflict management was having on the norm requiring marital co-residence—a norm noticed, for the most part, in its breach.

By the late sixties, anthropologists noted conceptual difficulties with definitions of the family that assumed the necessity of common residence.[1] Arguing that household and kinship are logically and empirically distinct categories (a household is a group of people living in the same home, while a family is a kinship or relational concept; see Bohannon, 1968; Bender, 1967; Stephens, 1963), they stressed the importance of separating

Dr. Gerstel is an Assistant Professor of Sociology at University of Massachusetts at Amherst, MA and Dr. Gross is University Professor of Sociology and Women's Studies at Governors State University, Park Forest South, IL.

the concept of household and family. Bender's assessment is typical: "There are numerous societies in which families do not form households and even more instances in which households are not composed of families." (Bender, 1967:493. See also Skolnick, 1978 and Leibowitz, 1978.) Spouses who maintain separate residences in the U.S. also speak to the reconceptualization of what constitutes a family unit. Scholarly research about such couples (Kirschner and Walum, 1978; Gerstel, 1979; Gross, 1980a) recognizes that residential separation of spouses is not without historical and cross-cultural precedent (e.g., war, Hill, 1949 and McCubbin et al., 1975; immigration, Handlin, 1951; imprisonment, Schneller, 1975; seasonal work, Abbott, 1976). In fact, Gross and Gerstel have developed a typology which classifies the variety of couples who live apart (Gerstel and Gross, 1981). Yet both they and the journalists who featured the lifestyle still acknowledge something "new" about this variant of separation: a wife's acquisition of career-enhancing opportunities equal to those of her husband. The lifestyle bore witness to the decade's determined effort to wrestle with the tensions spawned by liberationist yearnings on the one hand, and deeply felt intimacy needs on the other. In this climate, women's newly encouraged, and to some extent realized, aspirations for educational and occupational equity translate into domestic decisions to break with tradition in the service of both spouses' career goals. Research about these couples, dubbed variously "commuter," "long-distance," or "two-location" families, is the subject of this review.

The paper is organized into four main sections dealing with (1) definitions and incidence, (2) the effect of background characteristics on the choice and experience of commuting, (3) the consequences of establishing separate homes, and (4) conclusions about the viability, future research needs and policy implications of the two-residence marriage.

Commuters: Definition and Incidence

Discussion of dual career families in the pioneer work of Rapoport and Rapoport (1971 and 1976), and Holmstrom (1973), and most recently Hall and Hall (1979), Rice (1979), Pepitone-Rockwell (1980) and Skinner (1980) typically alludes to the tensions created by divergent demands for geographic mobility. Commuting is referred to as a possible "solution" to this problem (Nadelson and Nadelson, 1980). However, there are few data-based analyses of the circumstances surrounding actual decisions to live apart or the effects of choosing to do so. To date, results from five empirical investigations of this phenomenon comprise the data base for this lifestyle (Gerstel, 1979, 1978a, 1978b, 1978c, 1977; Kirschner and Walum, 1978; Gross, 1978, 1980a, 1980b; Farris, 1978; and Ortner, Sullivan, and Crossman, 1980).[2] In addition, several speculative papers analyze potential problems and implications of this marital form (Allen and Wilkie, 1976; Douvan and Pleck, 1978; and Pour-El, n.d.).

The maintenance of two separate households appears to be the common operational definition which researchers have used in all of these studies. Only two researchers further specify a minimum length of separation. Gerstel required that couples spend at least three days a week apart (1978c). Gross specified that they lived apart at least four days at a time (1980a).

Gross (1978) notes that the way in which couples separate differs. Typically, one spouse leaves a residence both had previously shared. Occasionally both relocate in different cities, e.g., one takes a new job while the other enters graduate school leaving both without a shared base to which either may return. More rarely, couples reside in two separate homes from the very beginning of their marriage.

Since all of the studies are based on non-random samples, and since no baseline data exist on the subject, existing research does not allow estimates of population parameters of such couples. Kirschner and Walum (1978) argue that census definitions preclude the possibility of estimating population parameters since they build co-residence into the definition of a marriage and define singles as those living with unrelated persons. However, Gross (1980a) notes that journalistic attention, so often a barometer of what is new and increasingly prevalent, confirms the view that the lifestyle's incidence is increasing. From the mid-seventies on, articles on the topic have appeared frequently in feature sections of large and small newspapers and magazines.[3] Despite the inability to estimate population frequencies, most authors base their expectations of the lifestyle's increasing prevalence on projections from several social trends: (1) more married women entering professional occupations which may produce mobility demands at variance with their husbands' careers (Gerstel, 1977; Gross, 1980a; Kirschner and Walum, 1978); (2) tighter job markets which force people to relocate (Gerstel, 1977); (3) greater equality within marriage which results in more attention to wives' career demands (Gross, 1980a; Gerstel, 1978b); and (4) increasing emphasis on individualism—a value which recognizes each spouse's right to pursue rewarding and self-actualizing pursuits (Ortner et al., 1979). As Gerstel (1977) suggests, this is an American value with a long history of application to husbands. What is new is its simultaneous application to wives.

Though the motivation to commute may be linked to a new recognition of the wife's previously blocked opportunities, the actual decision to commute is rarely a well conceived, planned reaction to such impediments (Farris, 1978 and Gerstel, 1978c). Rather, couples report a general lack of conscious decision-making preceding the plan to live apart. Typically, one or the other would begin an application process—for a new job or entrance to graduate study—without much discussion of what a favorable response to such application might mean for their shared lives.

Then when the desired position materialized and the actual decision to relocate was made, the fact of impending separation precipitated discussion of what living apart, taken more or less as a given, would entail. The lack of a conscious preliminary decision-making process reminds one of the path to voluntary childlessness described by Houseknecht in this volume. Such couples, she says, do not decide at an early age to remain childless. Rather they make their decision after they have developed a lifestyle they do not want to give up. Thus, for both types, the decisions emerge out of the logic of their lives as they have led them. To act otherwise would be to invalidate their previous choices and experiences.

Demographic Characteristics and Their Effect on the Choice and Experience of Commuting

A "middle-class" phenomenon

All of the studies to date on commuters suggest that the large majority of these spouses are well-educated, affluent professionals (Farris, 1978; Gerstel, 1977; Gross, 1980a; Kirschner and Walum, 1978). Over 90% had completed at least some graduate work. With such high levels of education, they tend to be involved in prestigious, high ranking occupational positions as academics, journalists, doctors, engineers, lawyers, and executives. In fact, in every study, over one-half of the respondents are academics. The skewedness of the occupational distribution—in particular the high proportion of academics—may be due in part to the "snowball" method used by all these researchers to gain a sample population, i.e., academics know or have access to other academics. However, there is some reason to suspect that these samples nonetheless do represent the commuting population. As Gerstel (1977) and Gross (1980a) point out, the flexibility of the academic work schedule, the relatively high degree of discretion most faculty have over time and place of work, and the often solitary conditions of this work may ease the establishment of commuting for academics relative to other occupational groups. Given these high levels of educational and occupational status, most of these couples also have high incomes. In not one of the studies did a single commuter couple have less than $18,000 in family income. The median family income ranged from $30,000 to $40,000. Clearly, this marital form is a middle or upper-middle class phenomenon. In fact, many families simply do not have adequate income to establish separate homes. Travel and long distance phone calls are a considerable expense as are costs of a second residence. Also, these couples may view hired help as necessary, especially if there are children.

Thus, while it is clear that couples must be relatively affluent even to establish a two-residence marriage, one of the greatest burdens of this lifestyle is the financial drain that it imposes (Gross, 1980a; Kirschner and Walum, 1978). In fact, using a cost-benefit analysis, Gerstel (1978b) found that though one partner obtained a better job by moving away from her/his spouse, the added income from that job was typically less than the total cost added by the commuting arrangement. This analysis suggests that commuters tend to be highly committed professionals who do not work primarily for a wage but rather because they view their work as a "central life interest."

Marital and Familial Characteristics

The research on commuters also found similar marital and familial conditions characterizing their samples. All found a mean age of from mid to late 30s, with a range, across studies, from 25-67 years. For the most part, these are not newlyweds; over half of all the commuters had been married more than nine years. Because of this age distribution, forty to fifty percent of the couples included in the samples had children.

These familial characteristics—number of years married and presence of children—influenced the experience of the commuter spouses. Both Gerstel (1977) and Farris (1978) suggest that for those in the child-bearing stage of life, especially when children are very young, commuting is far from an optimal arrangement. Many of the commuters without children said that they did not think they would commute with children. Yet, as indicated above, some parents did set up two separate homes. For a variety of reasons, they tended to find the commuting situation far more stressful than those without children. Most felt guilty breaking up their family home.

Those parents not only feared for their sons and daughters but often had the sense that they were missing vital daily parts of their children's development. Moreover, there was an asymmetrical increase in workload for the parent left with the child, typically, though far from always, the wife. Also, with children in the home, the spouses' already limited time with one another was even further reduced. And to make matters worse, Farris (1978) suggests that many of the parents had difficulty arranging childcare, particularly when either the child or the caretaking parent became ill. Finally not only did the parents have to deal with their own sense of loss and guilt, some simultaneously faced social pressures from other adults who questioned their adequacy as parents (Gerstel, 1978c). Such pressures serve to compound the anxiety that the commuter parents already felt. In terms of valued outcomes, Gross (unpublished data) found that fathers who remained with their children spoke of greater closeness, of being able to "get to know them better."

Gerstel (1978c) suggests that many of the commuters developed rationales to cope with their sense of guilt, stressing the quality rather than the quantity of child care. The use of this rationale aligned these parents with a position taken by many contemporary professional women (Van Mering, 1971). Others suggested that they were providing their children with a positive alternative role model. Many spoke of the benefits to their children of the necessary independence implied by the commuter arrangement. Such an ideology helped commuter parents cope with their atypical life situations. But it did not fully abolish the problems of parenting while apart.

Just as the research has shown that the absence of children facilitated the commuter arrangement, all of the studies found that the longer the couples were married, the less stressful they found separation (Gross, 1980 a,b; Kirschner and Walum, 1978; Gerstel, 1977; Farris, 1978). In fact, Gross (1980a) suggests that a distinction between younger "adjusting" couples and older "established" couples is particularly useful for an analysis of those dual-career couples who live apart. Younger couples have not been together long enough to see themselves as a solid reality or to have developed a trust based in a long, shared history. They are still adjusting to marriage. Simultaneously, these young couples must struggle over new issues of career ascendancy, asking: whose career concerns shall predominate? That is, not only are they in the process of establishing a sense of "we-ness" as a couple, but they have not yet firmly established professional identities in which they can experience confirmed competence.

In contrast, the "established" older couples, having endured as a marital unit, possess a backlog of experiences on which they can rely to stabilize their ongoing relationship. Moreover, these older couples recognize that they are finally correcting a previous imbalance in which the husband clearly had priority in the professional domain. They feel it is now the wife's "turn." Consequently, older couples acknowledge less strain than do the younger "adjusting" couples.

Only one of the studies (Gerstel, 1978c) deals with the issue of divorce. Gerstel interviewed a small number of commuters (N = 7) who subsequently divorced. All of these spouses said that though the establishment of two separate homes may have led them to obtain a divorce more quickly than if they had remained in a single home, the geographic separation was not itself a key factor in the actual decision.

Commuting Characteristics

With regard to the characteristics of the commuting situation itself, all of the research suggests a diversity of patterns. First, the number of years couples have lived in separate homes varied from as little as three months to as much as fourteen years. Second, the distance the spouses traveled between the two homes ranged, across studies, from 40-2700 miles. Third, in large part because of the range in distance apart, couples also varied widely in the amount of time they were able to spend in a single residence. In all studies, at least half of the couples were apart less than one week at a time. The remainder reunited from once every other weekend to less than once a month. Finally, the couples varied in the regularity of their reunions: some reunited every weekend without question while others came together whenever their schedules "permitted" them to do so.

While the studies found this wide divergence of commuting conditions, their findings tend to converge with regard to the effect of these conditions. Not surprisingly, the longer the distance traveled, the more burdensome and stressful the partners find the commute. Increased distance results both in increased cost (for phone and travel) and increased time and energy outlay. And, most importantly, the increased cost, time and energy required for the greater distance traveled tended to mean that spouses spent more time apart (Kirschner and Walum, 1978; Gerstel,

1977). When the time apart increases, so, too, does the dissatisfaction with commuter marriage. Gerstel (1979) suggests that there is a boundary on the amount of time that can be spent apart without serious cost to the relationship. Most couples who were apart only a week, or even two, found the situation tolerable and even in some ways beneficial. While those who lived apart for more than a month at a time were much more likely to find the situation extraordinarily stressful. In fact, a month—as the limit on possible separation—was mentioned again and again in the interviews. The commuters seemed to feel that if they were apart a month or more, they began to develop "separate worlds" or that their marriages began to resemble non-marriages. They no longer felt in touch with their spouses or felt that they had a unique relationship that provided an order to their lives.

Gross (1980b) suggests that in addition to the *duration* of separation, the *pattern* of separation also affects the quality of the commuting experience. Irregular regrouping, or reuniting when either spouse's schedule permits, challenges the relationship in a different way from those regrouping regularly. Couples who see each other every weekend have a pattern of separation and regrouping that roughly parallels the work-leisure pattern for most of society. That is, they are away from each other while others are working and together for the weekend which they, like other couples, are able to devote to activities they can do together. Without this regular pattern which resembles the lives of their dual-career counterparts, commuter spouses who regroup irregularly report that they feel "awkward" or "strange" when they come together. Some couples attach important symbolic meaning to weekend reunions. It signifies solidarity and continuity to the marriage (Gerstel, 1978). Finally, weekly regrouping couples who do not build up impossible expectations for their time together and who adapt readily to their routines, even taking comfort in their regularity.

In sum, the studies provide a consistent portrait of the enabling conditions for a commuting lifestyle. These findings suggest that commuting is likely to be least stressful when: 1) couples have adequate, if not high, incomes or financial resources; 2) spouses have intense career motivations or view work as a central life commitment; 3) couples are not newlyweds but have been married enough years to share a history which provides a "taken-for-granted" stability; 4) children are not yet or no longer in the home, and 5) spouses reunite regularly on weekends.

What if a couple has the best possible conditions? Even under optimal conditions research suggests that there are still disadvantages entailed in setting up two homes. Let us now turn to positive and negative consequences resulting from the establishment of commuter marriages.

Consequences of Commuter Marriage

Consequences for Careers and Daily Work Lives

The most obvious benefit that spouses, in particular wives, obtain from establishing two homes are those of career mobility and development (Farris, 1978; Kirschner and Walum, 1978; Gerstel, 1978b; Pour-El, n.d.; and Douvan and Pleck, 1978). The career gains for both spouses stand in high contrast to the career losses often entailed in an intact residential unit. For these spouses, like most other professionals, the husbands' jobs had carried greater weight than the wives' in determining the location of their joint residence. (For discussions of family mobility patterns among dual-career couples, see Linn, 1971; Holstrom, 1973; Duncan and Perucci, 1976; Ferber and Huber, 1979). Most commuter couples had, in the past, followed the husbands' careers (Gerstel, 1978c). The wives were unable (or unwilling) to move in response to their own employment opportunities. As a result, only the husbands followed an orderly career plan, moving to maintain or advance employment opportunities. In contrast, the wives faced grave barriers in formulating and achieving career goals while they shared a single home. As a result of this traditional pattern of geographic mobility, some of the wives faced unemployment. In a few cases, the informal (or even formal) application of anti-nepotism rules kept them out of the only employing institution in the area where their husbands had found work. If the wives did not remain unemployed altogether while still sharing a single family home, many could only find part-time jobs or jobs below the rank they could have obtained in another area. Some spoke angrily of the "exploitation" they had been subject to as members of a captive labor force.

The establishment of two separate homes, then, results in occupational gains. By setting up the commuter arrangement, both spouses are able to pursue their career paths equally, obtaining full-time professional employment consistent with their prior training, aspirations, and levels of skill.

Spouses choose to establish two homes so that they can both pursue orderly careers while remaining married. Thus, it comes as no surprise that the primary benefit they enjoy is that of occupational mobility. But these are not only gains to the spouses' careers. Their separation also has effects on daily work. Away from family pressures, the need for detailed daily planning diminishes. These husbands and wives experience a freedom which comes from not needing to dovetail each other's schedules around such constraints as meal time, recreation, or sleeping patterns. The freedom or simplification of daily lives allows them to concentrate more fully on their work if they so desire. Because their time is so compartmentalized, work often comes to dominate their "single" existences (Farris, 1978; Kirschner and Walum, 1978; Gerstel, 1977; Gross, 1980b).[4]

This increase in time spent on work is not viewed by everyone as beneficial. It is for the commuters. They are intensely involved in their professional lives, highly motivated and oriented to work as a "central life interest." Moreover, Kirschner and Walum (1978) suggest that commuters intensify their focus on work and achievement as justification for their unorthodox living arrangements. Thus, commuting reinforces the very orientations which are likely to sustain it as a marital form.

Yet Gross (1980b) finds that even for these professional spouses, there exists a concomitant response usually unconnected to the one suggesting separation increases work productivity. This response indicates a diminished capacity to work as concertedly or purposefully as they might like. Respondents commented: "I find I waste a lot of time" and "I don't get down to business the way I'd like." The diminished concentration may be evidence for the importance of marriage as a meaning-giving unit or as an institution that facilitates purposeful action by providing an individual with ". . . the sort of order in which he can experience his life as making sense" (Berger and Kellner, 1977).

The threat to this marital sense-making function may be especially important for couples who do not reunite in a single home on a regular basis where shared space as well as shared time sustain the "reality" of their lives (Gross, 1980b). For those separated in time and space, the ability to concentrate fully on purposeful work seems to decline. Thus, a diminished capacity to work productively may mitigate the increased productivity that results from not needing to dovetail with spouses' schedules.

Gerstel (1978) suggests that the inability to concentrate uninterruptedly may be more characteristic of commuter husbands than commuter wives. The wives had been the ones who provided the stable retreat or sanctuary in the home for their husbands and in doing so, served to relieve strains that impeded their husband's intense work involvement. Without the wife to manage intruding demands, the husbands often discover an inability to work as productively as they would like. Her data suggest that wives were much more likely than the husbands to increase the amount of professional work they did and much less likely to decrease their professional output.

Consequences for the Couple's Relationship

All of the research on commuters finds that residential separation is consequential for marital relationships. Commuters themselves take conventional marriage as the point of reference from which they assess their own non-traditional marriages. These couples stand as outsiders looking in, actively aware of what they once had but now miss. Also they are aware of what they now have but once lacked. The costs and benefits of commuter marriage provide us with insights into contemporary conventional marriage.

Most generally, these separated spouses are aware that living together creates a taken-for-granted intimacy. This is an intimacy of routine that has been widely criticized for its production of boredom, or worse, of despair. But commuters, because they live apart, experience a renewed sensitivity to the needs that such routines fulfill.

First, these spouses miss "trivial," everyday talk. They find they are unable to discuss family matters casually, to share and interpret one another's daily experiences, or to relate jokes and impressions of the day's events (Gerstel, 1977; Kirschner and Walum, 1978; Gross, 1980b). In order to cope with this inadequacy in their daily conversations, some keep diaries or tapes for their spouses and most call one another frequently. These phone conversations reduce loneliness and provide a sense of security, as well as limited emotional support. But they are considered a poor substitute for daily conversations. Commuters say they are keenly aware of both the cost of telephoning and lack of visual cues. As a result, they tend to summarize their experiences and discuss practical concerns rather than the much missed review of their daily lives (Gerstel, 1978c). Gross (1980b) suggests that without small talk, commuters lose the confirmation that helps produce the ordered world typically entailed in a marital relationship. As a result, some commuter couples—especially young couples without a solid base—fear they will move apart or that they are placing their relationship in jeopardy (Gross, 1980b; Farris, 1978).

Second, Gerstel (1978b) found that couples lamented their inability to share planned leisure activities. This loss was, of course, compounded the longer they lived apart. Many had planned leisure activities together only on weekends even before they set up two homes, just as most dual-career couples do (Rapoport and Rapoport, 1976). It is those couples who see one another less than once a week who generally face a sizeable decrease in shared leisure. However, almost all of the commuters suffer a loss with regard not to formal but to impulsive, unplanned recreation or the daily relaxations that come with sharing a single home. They speak, for example, of not being able to take a spontaneous walk with their spouse. Many speak of missing the shared dinner hour. While enjoying the freedom to sit down to eat at any time with any food they choose, commuters often speak of dinner as the loneliest time of the day. Time that had been conceived as routine, regular "family time" was now the period when their aloneness was felt most acutely.

Equally important is the loss of shared non-activities (Gerstel, 1978b). Commuters, because they are apart much of the time, focus on one another intensely when they come together. They cannot just "be" together and, during their solitary weeks, miss the mere presence of the other. An ability to sit quietly in the same room or same home with one another seems to obviate feelings of loneliness while providing a sense of security or stability. Commuters, by and large, often yearn for such shared non-activity provided by a single residence home.

The absence of both daily conversation and non-activity jeopardizes the taken-for-granted quality of their relationship. Even more fundamentally, commuters miss the common base that is their "home" where the sharing of daily trivia and activity/non-activity typically occurs. Gross (1980b) suggests that when they reunite away from their old shared "turf," they are unable to relax. Their reference to "re-entry problems" is evidence that they miss the familiarity, the sense of being "in place" that a shared home or living together provides. The home provides a sense of spatial interconnectedness; its absence calls into question the order-constructing quality of the marital relationship.

Though they lose and miss the daily intimacy that they understand as marriage, commuter couples are partially compensated for that loss by other changes in their relationship. Research on these two-residence couples suggests that when they reunite, both marital partners invest themselves in their relationship: they do not waste their time on other less important obligations. Their relationship is given priority (Kirschner and Walum, 1978). They allocate their time together in recognition of the fact that they must spend what time they have together wisely if the relationship is to withstand the injury to it that limited time periods impose (Gross, 1980b). Gerstel (1977) reports that many spoke of a sense of rediscovery: "We just don't take each other for granted anymore. Like things you strictly passed over, you notice again." Many were fighting less over tremendous trifles: "I don't get provoked when he leaves dishes in the sink. And he doesn't yell when I leave the cap off the toothpaste." Almost all spoke of heightened communication: "I miss having somebody to talk to every night when I come home. But when we finally see each other, we're like faucets that won't turn off." As Gerstel suggests, commuter marriage and conventional marriage are—in this respect—mirror images. By living together, couples obtain intimacy but such intimacy may yield disenchantment or frustration. By living apart, couples rediscover each other at the cost of daily intimacies. Here, the costs and rewards of residential separation expose a basic, perhaps irreconcilable, dilemma of conventional marriage.

However, we should not confuse the heightened companionship that commuters obtain with the romantic love associated with the beginning of affairs. Most spouses suggested that commuting resulted in an unwelcome reduction in the frequency of sexual intercourse without a compensating increase of passion or intensity (Gerstel, 1978b; Pour-El, n.d.). Some spouses even experienced a decline in the intensity of their lovemaking: they were tired, felt pressured to have sex, or needed time to readjust. More, Gross (1980b) found that some couples brought to their relationships inflated expectations which, when not met, marred the satisfaction of reunions. Because their time together is clearly bracketed off from "other time," this very distinctiveness makes their periods together more vulnerable. They are cognizant of "spoiled time" together in ways co–resident couples are probably not.

Researchers have not only found that the emotional components of marriage change with commuting. Studies of this lifestyle also suggest that a separation of the marital home induces a transformation of the division of household labor. Most of the couples become less traditional in their handling of domestic chores (Farris, 1978; Pour-El, n.d.; Gerstel, 1978b). In fact, Farris (1978) found a critical factor enabling couples to commute was the willingness of both spouses to abrogate traditional ideas of the wife/mother role. Before commuting most of these couples, like most dual-career co-resident couples, allocated primary responsibilities for household work to the wife. In contrast, when commuting began, there was of necessity a redistribution of these chores. Wives commented with pleasure on the tasks they no longer had to do and many spoke of being freed from household management. As a result of such redistribution, commuting is an equalizing force in the domestic division of labor. Women do less because they had done more in the past, while men do more because they had previously done less.

In addition, there are changes in domestic work which both spouses experience similarly. Gross (1980a) and Gerstel (1978b) found that both husbands and wives discovered an expanded sense of competence with regard to domestic duties, in particular those that have been traditionally defined as sex-linked. For example, wives learned that they could fix dripping faucets, mow lawns, and change tires. Husbands learned to cook or sew on buttons. Previously, before living apart, many had felt dependent in these areas, defining them as their spouse's area of expertise. The shared home, by the very success of its domestic division of labor, had produced an inability to move outside of domestic roles. The single residence marriage, by promoting a specialized division of labor, is a training ground for incapacitation (Gerstel, 1978b). But precisely because the domestic division of labor breaks down in commuter marriage, this alternative arrangement produces a new sense of effectiveness.

Research also suggests that the equalization of domestic work occurred in combination with a lowering of household standards by both husbands and wives (Farris, 1979; Gerstel, 1978b). For many of the husbands, tasks previously performed by their wives remained incomplete for longer periods of time. Many women, often to their own surprise, also found that their household standards were lower. For women, in particular, geographic separation seems to bring a transformation of needs (Gerstel, 1978b). Their comments suggest that much of the domestic burden appears to come from the pressure to act like a "good wife." These obligations are attached to the marital status. But they are fully activated only when both spouses share a single home. Wives feel a sense of responsibility, perhaps even a desire, to care for their husbands: to provide a real meal instead of a quick snack and to keep a neat *family* home. The commuters' comments suggest that it is not typically the husband who asks for high household standards. Rather, the wife often feels household chores to be a responsibility regardless of any overt demands, to meet her own self-image. But while this is a self-image, it is an image of herself in relationship to her husband. When apart from her husband, the wife's dinner and housecleaning can wait. She thinks of herself outside of her role as a wife and this, in turn, implies a reduction of household duties and standards.

However, these gains for women are not without their concomitant costs. Gross (1980a) found that the commuter wife experiences a certain amount of guilt attached to the recognition that her specialness in this regard causes her husband disadvantages relative to other husbands. Her sense of advantage is mitigated and undermined by this attendant guilt, leaving her with a burdensome, perplexing sense of somehow wronging him. Again, we see that the very benefits of the two-residence marriage are simultaneously understood as costs by those spouses who have only the conventional marriage to take as their standard of comparison. Part of the strain of commuting results from the discrepancies they sense from what is normative or what "should be."

Relationships with Others: Kin, Friends, and Lovers

As a result of the decreased interaction between spouses, do commuters' relationship with others—with kin, with friends, or even with lovers—increase in frequency or intensity? With regard to kin, Kirschner and Walum (1978) found that many male and female commuters were denigrated by members of their extended families. Farris (1978) found that for some, the greatest strain in the social network occurred in the relationship to the husband's parents, who were overtly disapproving, especially when they lived close by and young children were involved. Parents, too, take the conventional marriage as their standard and, in so doing, see their commuter children as negligent.

Moreover, most of the research suggests that partners who establish two separate homes face constraints in forming and maintaining relationships with friends (Gerstel, 1977; Gross, 1980a; Farris, 1978). Many friends assume a commuter marriage is one in trouble or one about to dissolve (Kirschner and Walum, 1978). Others express disapproval and, in so doing, strain the friendship (Gross, 1980b; Farris, 1978). However, the breaking of ties does not come simply from friends' skepticism or disapproval. As with previous research on the divorced (Weiss, 1979) and on widows and widowers (Lopata, 1973; Gerber, 1977), research on commuters suggests that the presence of two spouses in the home is required for the maintenance and development of friendship ties. When spouses are apart, many married couples exclude them because they are a threat or do not fit in (Gerstel, 1977; Kirschner and Walum, 1978). With the smaller number of singles, commuters share little in common (Gerstel, 1977; Gross, 1980). As "married singles,"they are unable to form independent ties (Farris, 1978), although Kirschner and Walum found a few exceptions to this pattern among some commuter wives who seemed able to form "support networks" with other sympathetic women. Moreover, Farris (1978) found that one major drawback of commuting to the

job is exclusion from the local "scene." The commitment of the commuter to the work organization and to colleagues is sometimes questioned, and this may have an adverse effect on the individual's career
future at that organization. Finally, when commuter spouses are together,
they generally feel that the intensity of their own interactions will be
reduced if others are included. They jealously guard the privacy of their
already limited reunions (Gerstel, 1977; Kirschner and Walum, 1978).

Gerstel (1977) suggests that these findings indicate that there are structural constraints that preclude attachments to others even when individuals
have the desire and time to form them. The "coupledness" of the social
world, the segregation of singles and marrieds, the localism of employing
institutions, and the priority of the marital relationship serve as constraints undermining individuals full use of affective energy. For married
adults, integration into social networks is not as individuals but rather as
members of marriages. Consequently, when spouses are apart they are
simply left with fewer active social bonds.

But what of extra-marital affairs? Commuters suggested that they were
constantly confronted with the belief by others that they would discard
habits of monogamy and take advantage of their new found possibilities
for sexual freedom (Gerstel, 1979; Kirschner and Walum, 1978). So, too,
our popular images would have sailors meeting lovers in every port and
businessmen seducing their traveling colleagues. These images assume
that the barriers marriage erects to extra-marital affairs are a result of the
ability of partners to keep an eye on each other's behavior. However,
contrary to these images, commuters were not more likely to have affairs
after they set up two homes than before (Gerstel, 1979; Ortner et al.,
1980). To be sure, some of these commuters had sexual relationships
with others while living apart. But most of these had done so before they
lived apart from their spouse. And many—who had not taken lovers while
they shared a single home—did not do so when they moved apart. That
is, the large majority of couples continued to act as they had before
commuting. These spouses did suggest that they were more likely to
fantasize about such affairs when they lived alone. However, for most,
these fantasies were not translated into sexual activity. These findings
suggest that it is not physical proximity—or an ability for regular obser-
vation—that allows marriage to serve as a mechanism of social control.
Instead, the constraints that marriage imposes on sexual affairs are a result
of an internalized value system which precedes residential separation,
advocating fidelity which many spouses can—and do—carry with them.

Conclusion

The Viability of Commuter Marriage

Two distinctive views of commuter marriage emerge from the papers reviewed here. Kirschner and Walum (1978), Pleck and Douvan (1978), Ortner et al. (1980), and Pour-El (n.d.) are all enthusiasts of commuter marriage. Like other commentators on the burgeoning of "alternative lifestyles," they are celebrating the increasing diversity of American life. Unlike an older sociology of the family which argued for the functional necessity of a conventional, residentially intact nuclear family, these authors are suggesting that the rise of commuter marriage represents a welcome expansion of available choices for marriage and of personal freedom within marriage. They see it as a healthy adaptation to the tensions of conventional marriage with few costs to the individuals involved.

However, while we would hardly argue for an uncritical acceptance of conventional marriage, we find such an interpretation too facile. Although commuter marriage is surely a response to the tensions of conventional marriage, it also generates tensions of its own. As this review has shown, residential separation can heighten intimacy between spouses, yet also threaten the bonds which sustain that intimacy. It may equalize the relations between partners and increase each one's sense of mastery, yet at the same time threaten the sense of what "should be." Most importantly, it may open new opportunities for career advancement of both spouses but at the expense of a shared home which is often equally valued. This analysis suggests that commuter marriage is a forced choice, that its benefits will outweigh its costs only in specific situations, and that its costs are never entirely absent.

Commuters themselves view their situation as temporary even without a tangible job offer to indicate its likely end. This suggests that compensatory psychic mechanisms are at work. Commuters who say they are only living apart as a temporary solution are like the voluntary childless who put off inquiries about their childbearing intentions by saying that they may adopt at some future date. Both use the self-imagery of temporary deviance to counter disturbing views of their lifestyle. Labeling oneself a temporary deviant, then, may be a psychic adaption to a problematic situation. Viewing one's lifestyle as "temporary" makes the uneasiness consequent upon such attribution easier to dispel. In the language of labelling theory it is a mechanism to undermine and forestall the possibility of becoming a self- and publicly acknowledged deviant.

The fact that commuters resort to such temporizing is itself indication that they, too, do not regard theirs as "the best of all possible worlds." It is perhaps tolerable but more in the nature of a putatively necessary adaptation than one enthusiastically endorsed for its "obvious" benefits. As researchers we must attend to the complexity of responses and not make pronouncements about a lifestyle's advantages, without taking into account the considerable strains these very advantages may produce.

Commuter marriage is a rational response to endemic conditions of family life rooted in a tension between career advancement and a shared residence. But to suggest commuter marriage is a rational response is not to suggest that commuter marriage is an ideal family structure. Couples face conflicting demands, values, and expectations. They want to live in one home. But they also want jobs. And they face a relatively inflexible occupational system. As a result, they sacrifice an aspect of their family lives.

Needed Research

All of the studies reviewed here relied on data from non-random samples. What is needed now is a random sample comparing commuters and non-commuter dual-career couples. Gross' work (1980a) suggests that among younger couples career ascendancy conflict exacerbates other tensions produced by living apart. We need to know how such conflict is managed among dual-career couples who do not live apart. Is such conflict less of a problem when the costs of commuting do not compound tensions? Do single residence dual career couples develop techniques—either intra-psychic or structural—to cope with such tensions? Or does Gerstel's (1978c) point about the subordinacy of wives' careers among professional couples mean that such conflict exists though it is not acted upon in co-resident dual-career couples?

We also need to compare dual-career couples who live apart with other couples who spend significant periods of time away from each other. While Gerstel (1978a), Gross (1980a), and Kirschner and Walum (1978) all refer to the precedent in our society for living apart set by the many examples of couples who do separate regularly, e.g., professional athletes, pipeline construction workers, and actors, none of these authors questions the viability of these traditional forms of separated living.[5] Yet preliminary results from ongoing research with Merchant Marine families who endure lengthy separations suggests that these couples may also experience stress (Gerstel and Gross, 1981). Unlike commuting career wives, Merchant Marine wives have husbands who are highly traditional. These husbands do not entertain the possibility that their wives might have professional aspirations. Typically they do not want them to take paying jobs at all or even to be involved in other non-domestic pursuits. Their reason: the wife should be "available" to them when they do come home, even though this may be for just a few hours at a time once or twice a month. Wives in these families also describe tension-ridden interactions with their husbands over child-rearing, in part, because the father's extensive absence makes him a difficult parental model to incorporate into the family authority structure. These are just two examples which suggest that our assumptions about the viability of these older traditional forms of marital separation may have been unwarranted.

We should not expect marital separation to be manageable just because historical and contemporary precedent for it exists. At the very least, these findings indicate a need for research on the separation experience of these non-dual career couples in order to unravel the effects of residential separation from other individual and couple characteristics.

This research topic needs longitudinal designs to assess the long-term effects of commuting on the careers of each spouse, their marriage, and their family relationships. With respect to the latter, the study of children in these families is necessary to assess commuting's effect on their socialization and behavior.

Finally, of particular importance for its policy implication is research on employer's responses to commuters. We need to know about their preconceptions as well as their actual responses to their married employees who live apart. Successful commuting may in part depend on greater employer acceptance of this marital variant. The role of corporate systems in transferring employees to other locations thus creating a commuter marriage is another topic for research.

Policy Implications

Thus, two sets of policy directives are required. One set is preventive, suggesting ways to eliminate constraints that force couples to make the decision to live apart. The other is remedial, suggesting ways to help couples contend with the problems of separate residences. In terms of prevention, employers need to extirpate remaining vestiges of anti-nepotism rules (Allen and Wilkie, 1976). However, even with a diminution in informal anti-nepotism practices, we may expect tight job markets to continue to exert pressure on dual-career couples to live apart. For those who must make this choice, pressure must be put on employers to be sensitive to commuting employees' special problems. Allen and Wilkie (1976) point out the localism bias of some university communities is a provincial hold-over which no longer serves university interests. Given national (even international) scholarly networks and the possibility of speedy travel, academics need not be tied to geographic locales to meet either scholarly or institutional commitments. In fact, some would argue that a cosmopolitan—rather than local—orientation is far more consistent with the professional norms of an academic setting. Even more important because it applies to all varieties of professional couples is employer recognition of and accommodation to the special time constraints under which such couples live. Commuter couples need flexible work and vacation schedules. Here both Gerstel's (1978c) finding that a month apart is as long as couples find readily manageable and Gross' (1980b) consideration of the productivity depleting effect of long separations imply that employers will best be able to profit from the high productivity of commuting employees, if they facilitate frequent spousal reunions. And, of course, the many supports needed by other working couples, such as expanded child care services, apply to commuters as well.

A condition not set by employers but by federal governmental regulations also needs reexamination. Under current laws, these couples can extract few beneficial tax considerations to help them finance their expensive lifestyle. More generally, when state laws require a shared domicile their separation may invalidate one spouse's citizenship rights, e.g., jury duty and voting rights (Weitzman, 1978).

But beyond these remedial work-related suggestions, traditional sex role expectations still hound these seemingly unconventional and for the most part egalitarian couples. This means that more than work strictures need to change. Normative definitions of the "proper" marriage must be transformed. The fact that traditional definitions of "appropriate" spousal behavior still affect these couples means that what is needed is a generation weaned on non-sexist, non-traditional values about relations between spouses and between the sexes.

NOTES

1. In diverse sources, social scientists had defined the family as a unit which necessarily involves residential unity. Murdock, in his classical formulization, defined the nuclear

family as a "Social group characterized by common residence, economic cooperation, and reproduction" (Murdock, 1949:1). Schneider noted: ". . . a condition which is part of the definition of American kinship: the family, to be a family, must live together" (1968:33). And even according to the U.S. Bureau of the Census: "The term family refers to a group of two or more persons related by blood, marriage, or adoption and residing together in a household" (1976:3).

2. Results from the work of Ortner, Sullivan, and Crossman are unpublished and available to the authors of this paper only in draft form. For this reason, we are not able to cite this work extensively in this review: Also, as we were going to press we were alerted to another study in progress by Barbara B. Bunker and Virginia Vanderslice in the Department of Psychology at SUNY, Buffalo.

3. See Gross 1980a, footnote 1, for mid-seventies references. Since 1978 additional articles include: Rousuck, 1978; Moromarco, 1978; Rubel, 1980; Cantarow, 1980.

4. It should be noted that no study provides empirical evidence for actual changes in productivity.

5. Although analyses of families separated by crises (e.g., imprisonment, Pueschel and Maglia, 1977; war or military service, McCubbin et al., 1975) recognize problems associated with this marital structure, there is little research about the effects of those occupations long associated with marital separation. However, there is a recent *New York Times* article which documents the concerns of clinicians who deal with strains endured by Merchant Marine families in Scotland (Border, 1980). See also Robinson, 1978 for an analysis of the problems spouses of medical students endure as a result of extensive separation from their mates.

BIBLIOGRAPHY

Abbott, Susan,"Full-time Farmers and Weekend Wives: An Analysis of Altering Conjugal Rules." *Journal of Marriage and Family* (February 1976) 36:165-173.

Allen, Irving Lewis and Jane Riblett Wilkie, "Commuting Married Faculty Women and the Traditional Academic Community." *Sociological Symposium,* Fall 1976, 33-43.

Bender, Donald R., "A Refinement of the Concept of Household: Families, Co-Residence, and Domestic Functions." *American Anthropologist,* 69 (October 1967) 493-504.

Berger, Peter and Hansfield Kellner, "Marriage and the Construction of Reality: An Exercise in the Micro-Sociology of Knowledge." *Diogenes,* 46:1-25, 1964.

Bohannon, Paul, "An Alternate Residence Classification." Pp. 317-323 in Paul Bohannon and John Middleton (eds.), *Marriage, Family, and Residence.* Garden City, New York: Natural History Press, 1968.

Border, William, "Away-on-Work Husbands and Marital Strains." *New York Times,* November, 11-20, 1980.

Cantarow, Ellen, "A Marriage of Inconvenience: How to Manage a Long-Distance Marriage." *TWA Ambassador,* August, 31, 1980.

Douvan, Elizabeth and Joseph Pleck, "Separation as Support." Pp. 138-146, Robert and Rhona Rapaport (eds.) *Working Couples.* Harper and Row, New York, 1978.

Duncan, R. Paul and Carolyn C. Perucci, "Dual Occupation Families and Migration." *American Sociological Review,* 41 (April 1976): 252-261.

Farris, Agnes, "Commuting." Pp. 100-107, Robert and Rhona Rapaport (eds.) *Working Couples.* Harper and Row, New York, 1978.

Ferber, Marian and Joan Huber, "Husbands, Wives, and Careers." *Journal of Marriage and Family* 41 (May 1979): 315-325.

Gerber, Irwin, "The Widower and the Family." Pp. 335-337 in Peter Stein, Judith Richman, and Natalie Hannon (eds.), *The Family: Functions, Conflicts, and Symbols.* Massachusetts: Addison-Wesley, 1977.

Gerstel, Naomi, "Marital Alternatives and the Regulation of Sex." *Alternative Life-styles*, 2,2 (May 1979) 145-176.
———— "The Residential Basis of Social Networks: Commuter Marriage as a Test Case." Paper presented at the Eastern Sociological Society Meetings, 1978a.
———— "Commuter Marriage: Constraints on Spouses." Paper presented at the 73rd Annual Meeting of the American Sociological Association, San Francisco, 1978b.
———— "Commuter Marriage." Unpublished Doctoral Dissertation, Columbia University, 1978c.
———— "The Feasibility of Commuter Marriages." Pp. 357-367 in Peter J. Stein, Judith Richmond, and Natalie Hannon (eds.) *The Family: Functions, Conflicts and Symbols.* Addison Wesley: Reading, Massachusetts, 1977.
Gross, Harriet, "Dual Career Couples Who Live Apart: Two Types." *Journal of Marriage and the Family* (August 1980a) 567-576.
———— "Couples Who Live Apart: Time/Place Disjunctions and Their Consequences." *Symbolic Interaction,* (Fall 1980b) 69-81.
———— "Couples Who Live Apart: The Dual-Career Variant." Paper presented at the 73rd Annual Meetings of the American Sociological Association, San Francisco, 1978.
Gross, Harriet and Naomi Gerstel, "A Special Case of Dual-Career Families: Couples Who Live Apart." Paper presented at the Groves Conference on Marriage and Family, Mt. Airy, Pennsylvania, May, 1981.
Hall, Francine S. and Douglas T. Hall, *The Two-Career Family*. Reading, Massachusetts, Addison-Wesley, 1979.
Handlin, Oscar, *The Uprooted*. Boston: Little Brown, 1951.
Hill, Reuben, *Families Under Stress*. Westport, Connecticut: Greenwood, 1949.
Holstrom, Lynda Lytle, *The Two-Career Family*. Cambridge, Massachusetts, Schenkman Publishing Company, 1973.
Kirschner, Betty and Laurel Walum, "Two-Location Families: Married Singles." *Alternative Lifestyles* (November 1978) 513-525.
Lasch, Christopher, *The Culture of Narcissism*. New York: Warner, 1979.
Liebowitz, Lila, *Females, Males, Families: A Biosocial Approach*. North Scituate, Massachusetts: Dexbury, 1978.
Linn, E.L., "Women Dentists: Career and Family." *Social Problems* 18 (Winter 1971) 393-403.
Lopata, Helena Z., *Widowhood in an American City*. Cambridge, Massachusetts: Scheckman Publishing Company, 1973.
McCubbin, Hamilton I., Edna J. Hunter, and Barbara B. Dahl, "Residuals of War: Families of Prisoners of War and Servicemen Missing in Action." *Journal of Social Issues,* 31, 4, 95-109, 1975.
Moramarco, Sheila, "Marriage on the Run." *Dynamic Years,* December 19, 1978.
Murdock, George Peter, *Social Structure*. New York: Free Press, 1949.
Nadelson, Carol C. and Theodore Nadelson, "Dual-Career Marriages: Benefits and Costs." Pp. 91-109 in Fran Pepitone-Rockwell (ed.) *Dual-Career Couples*. Beverly Hills: Sage, 1980.
Ortner, John, Sullivan, Joyce, and Crossman, Sharyne M., "Long Distance Marriage." Unpublished paper.
Pepitone-Rockwell, Fran (ed.), *Dual Career Couples*. Beverly Hills: Sage, 1980.
Pour-El, Marian Boykan, "Spatial Separation in Family Life—A Mathematician's Choice." Unpublished paper.
Pueschel, Janet and Maglia, Ronald, "The Effects of the Penal Environment on Familial Relationships." *Family Coordinator* (October 1977) 373-375.
Rapoport, Robert and Rhona Rapoport, *Dual Career Families.* Harnondsworth, Eng. Penguin, 1971.
———— *Dual-Career Families Re-Examined*. New York: Harper & Row, 1976.

Rics, Donald, *Dual-Career Marriage: Conflict and Treatment.* New York: Free Press, 1979.

Robinson, David Owen, "The Medical-Student Spouse Syndrome:Grief Reaction to the Clinical Years." *American Journal of Psychiatry.* 135:8, 972-974, 1978.

Rousuck, J. Wynn, "Commuter Marriages: Apart But Together." *Baltimore Sun Magazine,* December 6, 1978.

Rubel, Nina, "Commuter Marriage: Working to Make it Work." *Champaign-Urbana, Illinois News-Gazette,* January 20, 1980 B-1.

Schneider, David, *American Kinship: A Cultural Account.* New Jersey: Prentice-Hall, 1968.

Schneller, D.P., "Prison Families: A Study of Some Social and Psychological Effects of Incarceration on the Families of Negro Prisoners." *Criminology.* 12:402-12, 1975.

Skinner, Denise, "Dual-Career Family Stress and Coping: A Literature Review." *Family Relations,* 29 (October 1980) 473-480.

Skolnick, Arlene, *The Intimate Environment.* Toronto: Little Brown: second edition, 1978.

Stephens, William N., *The Family in Cross-Cultural Perspective.* New York:Holt, Rhinehart, and Winston, 1963.

Turner, Ralph,"The Real Self: From Institution to Impulse." *American Journal of Sociology,* 81 (March 1976): 989-1016.

Van Mering, Faye, "Professional and Non-Professional Women as Mothers." Pp. 556-583 in Athena Theodore (ed.), *The Professional Woman.* Massachusetts: Schenkman Publishing Company, 1971.

Veevers, J.E., "The Moral Careers of Voluntarily Childless Wives: Notes on the Defense of a Variant World View." Pp. 367-380 in Peter J. Stein, Judith Richman and Natalie Hannon (eds.) *The Family: Functions, Conflicts and Symbols,* Addison-Wesley, Reading, Massachusetts, 1977.

Weitzman, Lenore, To Love, Honor and Obey: Traditional Legal Marriage and Alternative Family Forms. Pp. 288-313 in A.S. Skolnick and J.H. Skolnick (eds.) *Family in Transition,* Boston: Little Brown, 1978.

Wolf, Tom,"The 'Me' Decade."*New York,* 9 (August, 23, 1976): 26-40.

FOSTER PARENTHOOD: A NONNORMATIVE PARENTING ARRANGEMENT

Kathleen Sampson Eastman, PhD

Introduction

Because they have been with us since at least the nineteenth century, foster families are not usually conceptually linked with those alternative family forms that became more socially visible in the seventies. Yet, as we shall see, many of the social changes propelling other alternative family forms into existence also affect the composition and the future of these families. This analysis will (1) place the current trend toward specialization of foster homes in the context of historical changes and the development of foster families in the United States; (2) discuss sources of ambiguity in the foster parent role and (3) review issues associated with recruitment, selection and successful placements as well as legal shifts affecting foster families.

The Foster Case System: Development and Change

When it began in the late nineteenth century, the foster care system was loosely structured and served primarily to meet the needs of city youngsters whose parents suffered economic hardship. The Home Missionary Society of Philadelphia and the Children's Aid Society of Pennsylvania led the way in early placement efforts. From these early beginnings came two different placement philosophies. The Home Missionary Society of Philadelphia required natural parents to relinquish their rights—sever all ties with their children—and then the children were subsequently placed in indenture arrangements. This, therefore, made the new living arrangement permanent.

Dr. Kathleen Sampson Eastman is Lecturer in the Department of Sociology and Anthropology, New Mexico State University, Las Cruces, NM.

The Children's Aid Society of Pennsylvania chose not to indenture children. Rather they preferred the option of removing a child from his/her substitute home in case the child had received poor care, then the child could be returned home when their family's social and economic situation improved. This system allowed for reunification of family members and therein lay its strength. The indenture arrangement practiced by the Home Missionary Society of Philadelphia did not allow for this option. However, the Children's Aid Society's placements had the negative aspect of impermanence. Children were often placed in a board home only to moved again and again until the agency found someone willing to offer them a free home (Clement, 1979). With the passage of time both the indenture arrangement and the free home passed out of favor and the paid foster home was ushered in as the primary foster care arrangement.

Even though these early forms of foster care existed since the late nineteenth century, institutional care remained the primary mode of care until far into the twentieth century. It was the Social Security Act of 1935 which helped open the door to noninstitutional alternatives for children needing placement (Wyoming Social Services Manual, 1979). A movement began to develop against institutional care and toward foster care. The belief was that institutions were destructive to human personality and they failed to prepare youngsters placed within them for self-sufficiency and independence. The view was that institutions were not meeting the needs of children nor were they meeting the needs of society. A strong sentiment developed for children to grow up in a family setting, even if it was not their own family (Fanshel, 1960; Rose, 1962). With these changing societal attitudes and the financial backing of the Social Security Act of 1935, foster care in the 1950's emerged as the primary substitute care arrangement for children in the United States (Clement, 1979).

Since the 1950s the trend towards deinstitutionalization of children has continued. The foster family arrangement is a less costly arrangement than institutional care and has other presumed benefits (Wiltse, 1978). Philosophies of child rearing presently adhered to discourage institutionalization and encourage the trend toward community-based services and normalization of children. In 1972, the last year thorough documentation was kept as to the number of children in substitute care arrangements, there were 319,848 children in foster care; 248,512 in foster family homes; 6,589 in group homes; and 64,738 in institutions (Wiltse, 1978). These statistics indicate that foster family homes are the preferred mode of substitute care. And with the increased pressure to further reduce the institutional placements of children, one will find the foster home population further expanding in relation to the institutional category. More and more emotionally disturbed children, mentally retarded children, and adjudicated delinquents are being channeled into foster care. Foster homes are increasingly being asked to absorb children that in the past would have been institutionalized (Rose, 1962; Levine, 1972).

The foster care population is changing. In the early days of foster care children were primarily poor. Today, the children often come from economically deprived backgrounds but they also exhibit a range of difficulties not earlier seen in foster care (Pare & Torczyner, 1977). Poverty is no longer the only problem. "Within the last decade, the population of foster children has changed radically. . . . The vast majority of children are emotionally or physically handicapped" (Nebraska's Guide for Foster Parents, 1978).

In addition to an increase in children with serious emotional and developmental disorders placed in foster care there has been an increase in the number of youth who are status offenders. The juvenile justice system has also turned away from institutionalization as the preferred mode of treatment and has moved toward community -based services.

The category of teenage placements has mushroomed. Some teenagers are a product of foster homes but many have entered the system during their teen years having had conflictual relationships with their parents or difficulties with the law. These placements are a much more difficult challenge than the placements of the past. To attempt to deal with the severity of these problems, foster homes have become increasingly specialized and many have become group homes. In the 1970's, specialization became a reality.

Historically, the natural parents of children placed in foster care have been poor. Adverse social and economic conditions necessitated placement. Poverty was the root cause of placement, and no public relief existed. Also, most children placed were from single parent households largely headed by women. However, placement remained temporary and when the times got better the children were reunited with their families (Clement, 1979). Today, foster children are still primarily products of the poor and the majority come from single-parent, female-headed households (Schott, 1974; Kadushin, 1978; Finkelstein, 1980).

Torczyner and Pare (1979) found that characteristics of the natural home remain the most important reason for placement of children. Furthermore, they found that the children were likely to be returned home when the home situation improved. Today, as in the beginning of the foster care system, the financial and social resources of the natural parents are of paramount importance. Low-income status and single parent-hood seem to reduce the prospect of a child's return to his natural par-ents. This causes concern among child welfare professionals as the United States has a growing number of families that are single-parent families headed by women. Their children are at risk should the parent encounter financial difficulties or a breakdown in the social support system. The legal marriage, which was once viewed as so binding and so permanent, is no longer held in this light (Finkelstein, 1980).

With the weakening of ties between marital partners has come the difficult problem of what to do with the children. By and large one or both parents want the child and seek custody, or joint custody is sought. However, occasionally neither parent wants custody or responsibility of the child upon the dissolution of the marriage. In this case the child might enter foster care. As marital ties lessen there will be more children that find their way into foster care either because neither parent wants them or because the single parent given custody is incapable of meeting the child's needs. To counteract this tendency the Adoption Assistance and Child Welfare Act of 1980 provides financial incentives for agencies to redirect much of their energy toward assisting parents, rather than maintaining placement (Calhoun, 1980).

Foster homes have historically consisted of the two-parent traditional family. This trend continues today. Agencies prefer the two-parent sys-tem but will allow a single person to become a foster parent if that individual has "exceptional" qualifications. The single foster parent, however, would be limited to providing for a school-age child or a special needs child.

In the 1970s our society was a society in transition. No area of change impacted on the family more than the change in sex roles. Since it became common for women to enter the world of work in large numbers, foster care agencies had to address this issue of foster mother's employ-ment. Because "an increased commitment by wives to paid employment will result in fewer mothers with small children remaining at home," (Knox, 1980:147) agencies need to reexamine their policies toward foster mother employment or they will face an increasingly small pool of appli-cants.

The basic question has been: if a foster mother works can she provide good parenting to a foster child? One study by Kraus (1971) found that the foster mother who worked was successful at fostering as the mother who did not work. This study indicated that employment need not be viewed negatively and that the pool of potential foster parents need not be limited to nonworking mothers.

Many agencies are now allowing foster mothers to be employed if they are caring for school-aged children. Also, if agencies want to counteract the dwindling pool of potential applicants they must make foster parenthood attractive. Foster parenthood needs to gain status and become more financially remunerative. It needs to become a viable economic alternative to seeking out-of-home employment. The societal trend of women in the labor force is going to continue and agencies must come to terms with it either by accepting employed mothers into their foster home program or by increasing the benefits of foster parenthood. An increasing number of home providers will then view foster care as a viable alternative to out-of-home employment.

Specialization of Foster Homes

In the early days, foster homes were differentiated according to the length of placement, either as a permanent long-term arrangement or a more temporary short-term one. In recent times foster homes have not escaped the move to increased specialization, a process found in all sectors of society. Throughout the late 1960s and the 1970s, specialization of homes increased largely due to deinstitutionalization efforts. "Specialized foster care programs are a recent development in the field of family and child welfare . . ." (Russell and Silberman, 1978:403).

Throughout the literature there is much discussion of issues associated with specialized functions. Foster care placements vary according to the length of time of placement (temporary vs. permanent), the development stage of the child (adolescent or infant home), the disability of the child (mental retardation, emotional disturbance, or visual impairment) and the acceptability of siblings in the same home. Many of these homes differ from the traditional foster family home not only by specialization of function but also by being designated as group foster homes. They often have a minimum of six foster children and require special licensing and zoning procedures.

Some authors argue strongly that foster care is temporary care whereas others argue that foster care, is, in reality, not temporary care but rather long-term and all-too-often permanent care. Fanshel's (1971) research indicated that there is a major exodus of foster children from foster care within the first year of placement. Jenkins' (1967) data indicated that approximately half of all placements are under three months duration while 25 percent of the children's placements are of more than two years duration. These studies were the more optimistic ones regarding children's length of stay in foster care.

Maas (1969) found that only 24 percent of the children left foster care in less than three years. Rothschild (1974) found that 70 percent of the placements were of three or more years length. Glassberg (1965) reported that in 1961 in Philadelphia one-fourth of the children had been in foster care no less than seven years. And according to Claburn et al. (1976: 395), "studies of foster care have demonstrated conclusively that a large proportion of foster children remain in care in excess of five years, frequently for most of their childhood." Fashel and Shinn (1978) found that many children stayed in foster care approximately five years. Bryce and Ehlert (1971) found that the average length of stay for children was approximately three years. Maas (1969) argues that when foster care is of several years duration the concept of temporariness is not supported.

The variations in these studies suggest that foster care is both temporary and long-term. Within the child welfare system, there are children whose stay in foster care ranges from a few days to several months. These placements would readily be classified as temporary placements. However, there are also children within the foster care system who have gone through a multitude of foster homes until they have reached their age of majority. For them, foster care is clearly permanent care.

In the life of a foster family whether a child stays for a few months or a few years, the indeterminate length of stay creates a feeling of impermanence and temporariness. The foster family does not know how fully to incorporate the child into their family system as they do not know for how long the child is to remain. This vagueness about duration of stay is a source of considerable stress for foster families (Kline & Overstreet, 1972; Wilkes, 1974). According to Dinnage and Pringle (1967:29), "the fact that the likely duration of the foster situation is in many cases unknown . . . adds to the uncertainty and hence, insecurity, inherent in the whole framework."

Concerted efforts are now being made to reduce this ambiguity through such means as permanency planning and the use of contracts as well as a comprehensive review system (Atherton, 1974; Schott, Jr., 1974; Stein et al., 1977; Davies & Bland, 1978; Jones, 1978; Jones & Biesecker, 1980; Poertner & Rapp, 1980).

Homes are also classified according to the developmental stage of the child. Of the various living arrangements for teenagers, group foster care seems to be one of the most desirable arrangements. Adolescents experiencing placement must contend with both the crisis of placement and the crisis of adolescence (MacIntyre, 1970). Often the adolescent has been involved in a conflictual relationship with his family and may be better served by placement that does not call for him to closely interact with a family (Gordon, 1976). The group home has structure but allows more autonomy than a traditional foster home. For the adolescent, a group living situation with adolescent peers is often the preferred mode of care (Ellis, 1973).

It is often desirable to place siblings together; therefore, sibling homes are a valuable resource to the agency. Meyer (1969) holds that siblings should be placed together unless there is strong diagnostic evidence that would lead one to decide otherwise. Placing siblings together reduces the likelihood of emotional change (Aldridge & Cautley, 1976).

The 1970s ushered in a phenomenal amount of growth in group homes and specialized homes particularly for children with special needs. Staff in these homes often receive additional training and qualify for added financial remuneration.

Beginning in the late 1950s an increasing number of emotionally disturbed children were entering foster care (Naughton, 1957). The thrust toward deinstitutionalization furthered their entry into foster care. In recent years agencies have developed intensive treatment homes for children that have been severely abused (Harling and Haines, 1980). These children have emotional problems and agencies are becoming increasingly sensitive to the special emotional needs of foster children.

A significant number of foster children are diagnosed as mentally retarded as indicated by Schott's (1974) analysis of Iowa children. Schott found that of 5,481 foster children in care in 1973, 2,338 of them were below average in intelligence. Freeman (1978) finds foster homes to be a promising setting for many mentally retarded children who otherwise might be institutionalized. Freeman holds that real progress can be made with these children in such a setting. By expressions of love and warmth and intellectual stimulation they can achieve a higher level of functioning in both social and academic skills. Fanshel and Shinn were less optimistic (1978). In their study children in foster care did not make significant emotional and intellectual gains.

Historically, visually impaired children were often placed in either state schools or institutions. Today many of these children are cared for by natural or by foster parents who work with community-based schools and agencies to meet their social and intellectual needs (Moore, 1976).

Sources of Ambiguity in The Foster Parent Role

Foster parenting is a nonnormative parenting arrangement. When a child enters foster care, parental authority is shared by the natural parents, the agency, and the foster parents (Galaway, 1972). Hikel (1973) points out that sharing these parental responsibilities is unconventional. And because these parental responsibilities are not clearly differentiated and understood by all concerned, considerable role strain and ambiguity results (Kennedy, 1973). Furthermore, lack of role clarity makes for unhealthy family functioning (Barnhill, 1979). The need is for role clarity. The Bill of Rights for Foster Parents lists the need for a clear understanding of the role of foster parent and the respective roles of natural parent and child-placing agency (Garrett, 1970).

Eastman (1979) refers to foster families as systems having vague identity. Foster homes are known to suffer from a lack of role clarity and clearly defined norms. However, with the assistance of various court rulings (Katz, 1976) foster parents are attempting to define their roles, norms, and identities. With increased norm clarity and role definition greater satisfaction will come for foster parents and children. "Children reared in homes of norm clarity are found to be happier and more successful in adjusting to the norm requirements of school and play" (Monane, 1967:119-20). Also "Beavers found that when family members had clearly defined role boundaries, the members could achieve intimacy and empathy for one another. . . ." (Kent, 1980:148).

The earliest stages of foster parenting create the greatest amount of vague system identity. Foster parents are asked to fulfill roles that are not only new and unknown to them, but which are also ill-defined. This vague system identity can only add to the stress and breakdown of early placements of foster children that many studies find so common (George, 1970; Radinsky, 1970; Kay, 1971a; Levine, 1972; Aldridge & Cautley, 1975).

The lack of normative consensus also creates boundary confusion. What is the domain, cultural characteristics, competencies, and functions and other components of the foster care system, placement agencies and natural families. Although the foster family and the agency both attempt to screen children appropriate for placement in a particular foster home, 41 percent of all placements are unsuccessful. They are terminated before a child is ready to leave foster care (Festinger, 1975). This difficulty with inclusion and exclusion of children goes beyond physical incorporation of the child into the family system. Much more important is psychological incorporation of the child into the family.

The problem of lack of role clarity and responsible functions within defined boundaries is further compounded by the agency's unclear perception of the foster parent. Again and again the question comes up whether the foster parent is client or colleague (Lawder, 1964; Reistroffer, 1972; Jones, 1975). Foster parents are providers of a service and an extension of the child care staff. They are a valuable member of the child treatment team (Gabrovic, 1973). And yet foster homes are supervised and under agency control. The locus of control remains with the agency.

Foster parents clearly are not agency clients, yet they are aware of the agency's power over their lives. The agency has the power to license their home and to revoke it. The agency decides whether to place or remove a child. Foster parents may choose to accept a placement or request a removal, but their power is clearly less than the agency's power. Because of this power differential there are repeated efforts to remind agency staff that foster parents are not clients but rather providers of a service (Reistroffer, 1968; Daniels & Brown, 1973). According to Kline and Overstreet (1972) even when hired as agency staff, foster parents viewed themselves in the parenting role. In reality neither label applies fully: they are neither clients nor colleagues. Rather they are foster parents. According to Babcock (1965) foster parents are capable of distinguishing the difference between their parental relationship toward their own children and toward foster children. "They differentiated well what constituted a parental relationship to own children and a foster relationship to the foster children" (Babcock: 489).

Recruitment and Selection

When foster care originated in the nineteenth century, it was a casual arrangement. Advertisements expressing the need for foster parents ran in local newspapers and prospective foster parents found themselves with a foster child within a few hours after they made their request (Clement, 1979). In the 1980s applicants began to fill out application forms and provide references. Throughout the years, it has become an increasingly formal arrangement between agency and foster parents (Freund, 1976). Most foster parents today undergo extensive interviewing, health and safety inspections, and in some states (Arizona, Mississippi, Alaska, Nevada, Massachusetts, and New Jersey) foster parents must be cleared through the local police department. This is very different from the loosely structured beginning.

Some agencies have attempted to eliminate the formality of the process by experimenting with the selection method. One method being attempted with relative success is a self-selection method whereby prospective foster parents attend training sessions. Those that complete the training sessions are eligible to become foster parents. This selection method has proven to be highly successful (Stanley, 1971). Foster parents who have completed the training sessions begin their role as foster parents better trained than those foster parents who have only undergone extensive interviews. They also have a more positive attitude toward the agency. An added benefit, is that these families also have much better participation from foster fathers (Freund, 1976).

Other selection methods have used projective tests and psychiatric interviews in obtaining foster parents for emotionally disturbed children (Naughton, 1957). With group foster homes or "special needs" homes recruitment often takes place "in house." This allows parents for these "special needs" children to have previous experience with fostering (Freeman, 1978). These efforts seem to be beneficial to the applicants, the agency, and foster parents. Coyne (1978) found that in recruitment efforts, personal interaction between foster parent and applicant is a decisive factor in convincing others of the benefit of fostering. Also, mass media campaigns have been involved in recruitment. Though these may create overall awareness, they do produce actual parental applications. Sacks and Case (1958) found that with ads, one out of a hundred inquiries will materialize. They hold that foster parents are the best source of recruitment.

In policy manuals and foster parents handbooks, many states encourage the use of foster parents as recruiters (Georgia Foster Parent Manual, 1978; Kentucky Community Services Manual, 1978). A Canadian agency also experimented with hiring foster parents as part-time agency staff to recruit, screen, and train foster parents (Pedosuk & Ratcliffe, 1979). The real benefits of engaging existing foster parents in recruitment efforts is aptly stated by Gabrovic: "For the licensed foster family, there has been greater participation with the agency and the community; for the prospective foster family, there has been the opportunity to explore a program before becoming committed to it in a formal study; and for the agency, there has been the enrichment that comes from involving its foster parents in another phase of the total program" (Gabrovic, 1973:23). While the overwhelming evidence tends to indicate that foster parents are the best source of recruitment efforts, Drydyk et al. (1980) did find classified ads to be the most successful method for recruiting developmental foster homes. And Delgado (1978) found community and personal contacts to be the most effective means of recruitment.

Agencies must cope with the question of "where do we recruit for foster parents?" Agencies traditionally have restricted their foster homes to the middle-income range, the rationale being that these homes could best provide for an additional child and that these homes would be transmitting basic American values to the foster child. Low income homes were largely excluded because of their financial state. Now agencies are becoming more aware that these homes with limited financial resources may be able to offer the child other things that may be equally, if not more important, than financial resources. These homes may offer a child cultural ties, a sense of identity, and continuity with his past (Delgado, 1978; Garber et al., 1970). Agencies have even successfully placed children in ghetto homes. And Delgado's (1978) study would indicate that if a child is from the ghetto he might do better in a ghetto home than in a middle-class home. The child has fewer barriers to cross. Goldstein (1973) also supports providing a child a home with a similar heritage. She endorses Jewish children being placed in Jewish homes so as to be involved in Jewish holidays and traditions and to gain strength from knowing their heritage and identity as a people.

Although foster care is considered the most desirable resource for children needing substitute care, it remains extremely difficult to recruit new foster homes. This is true even though a New Jersey survey indicated that the general public had a positive attitude toward foster parenting (New Jersey Foster Home Developers Manual, 1976). In 1962, McCoy indicated that foster parents were often treated to one of two possible responses by the public: 1) they were viewed as kind and humanitarian or 2) they were viewed suspiciously as someone wanting to make money from their involvement. It is encouraging that by 1976 the attitudes are more positive than in 1962.

But even with more positive public attitudes, it is difficult to recruit new homes. In Glassberg's (1965) study the ratio of families accepted into the foster home program for the one year period of 1962-1963 was one approved home for every 16 inquiries. Sacks and Case (1968) found that only one home materialized for every 100 inquiries. One might assume incorrectly that the agency was rejecting applicants in vast numbers. Such was not the case. Rather the majority of those who inquired chose not to complete the application process; these individuals withdrew their applications if they had gone so far as to complete one.

Furthermore, once homes are recruited, it is difficult to maintain them in a foster home program. Research indicates that foster homes are particularly vulnerable to breakdown during or after the first placement (Radinsky, 1970; Levine, 1972). The first placement creates stress as foster parents are asked to assume an unfamiliar role. "It can be generally assumed that first placements are likely to be more stressful than placements coming later when the experience is less unfamiliar" (Kay, 1971a: 72). Many new foster parents do not adjust to the demands and stresses of foster parenthood and choose to end their involvement with the foster home program. George (1970) indicated that although the risk for foster home breakdown is high during the first year, it steadily diminishes over time. Eastman (1978) found that 30 percent of foster parents withdrew from the foster home program after having been involved in fostering for less than a year. Cautley and Aldridge (1973) come to the conclusion that becoming a foster parent is a difficult process. Four weeks after the initial placement only 20 percent of the foster parents were highly positive about the placement. Many found the role demanding or were disappointed. However, they did find that if the home remained in the program beyond the one year point, the foster parent began to speak more positively about fostering.

Agencies have come to recognize the difficulty in both recruiting and maintaining foster homes and many mandate orientation of new foster parents and require 15 hours of additional training per year for ongoing homes. Some agencies have begun to teach communication skills, value clarification, behavior modification, and listening skills. Guerney (1975) emphasizes the importance of communication skills. Penn (1978) endorses the use of behavior modification techniques. Stone (1978) encourages training in many areas that include: first aid, sexuality, and communication. Felker (1978) would hope that training programs would offer value clarification. Gross et al. (1978) call for increased teaching of basic child development in foster homes. In training programs, it is helpful to teach not only basic foster care concerns but also communication skills, behavior modification, and value clarification.

What attitudes do foster parents have regarding training? Drydyk et al. (1980) indicated that the foster parents were highly supportive and extremely positive toward the training experience they received. However, Hampson and Tavormina (1980) found few foster parents supporting the existing training program. Most of the foster parents they interviewed rarely attended. Training programs suffer from attendance difficulties, not only with foster mothers, but also with foster fathers. Of those foster parents who do attend training, the majority are mothers. Stone (1980) found that two-thirds of persons present were female. This coincides with the agency's method of dealing primarily with the foster mother (Lindberg & Wosmek, 1963). The foster mother continues to represent the foster family to the agency.

With the increased training emphasis, the value of such experiences have been investigated. Boyd and Remy (1978) find that training is indeed helpful to foster parents. Their findings indicate that with training: 1) unsuccessful placements were reduced; 2) probability of a desired placement outcome was increased; and 3) foster parents were more likely to remain in the foster home program.

Another mechanism that developed in the 1970s to aid and assist foster parents was the growth of foster parent associations. A national foster parent association was formed in the 1970s and so were a sizable number of state and local chapters. Foster parent groups have helped to raise foster parent consciousness. Groups provide strength to individuals by bringing together people that share common experiences and common concerns. Associations may also provide an educational function by providing their own series of programs and by encouraging foster parent participation in agency-sponsored events. Reistroffer (1968) found that participation enhanced parental skills and also provided a better understanding of the complexity of the entire foster care system. Reistroffer's groups drew heavily upon university personnel for expertise. Not only are foster parents becoming increasingly involved in support and educational groups but also in advocacy groups. Associations often are pressing for improved services or policy changes (Anderson, 1973). Foster parent advocacy may range from higher board rates to better clothing allotment systems to liability insurance coverage. Their advocacy position, while an additional resource for meeting the needs of the foster child, is a challenge to the agency. Some agencies view foster parent associations as one more pressure block with which to contend. Rosendorf (1972) indicated that social workers often resent foster parent demands and fear the pressure of the foster parent association.

Foster Home Studies Regarding Success and Satisfaction

Foster home programs throughout this country have had great difficulty maintaining their homes in their respective programs. Because it is important for the child's welfare to maintain placement stability, numerous studies have been made to examine the satisfaction of foster parents and the variables that relate to effective home functioning. The foster home satisfaction and success studies will be divided into three categories: those that relate to demographic, relationship, and personality variables.

Demographic Variables

Many foster home studies have attempted to determine whether demographic variables affect foster home satisfaction or success. Numerous studies (Parker, 1966; Fanshel, 1970; Mandell, 1973; Cautley & Aldridge, 1975; Rowe, 1976; Delgado, 1978) relate foster care variables to socioeconomic class. Whereas Row (1976) found that social class was unrelated to the quality of fostering, Parker (1966) indicated that the lower socioeconomic class was the most successful at fostering. Cautley and Alderidge (1975) report the opposite.

Mandell (1973) favored lower class for fostering because of their greater tolerance, but Fanshel (1978) expressed concern regarding the childrearing attitudes of the lower class. Delgado (1978) found that the important variable was not a particular social class but that the foster child and foster parent share a similar socioeconomic background. Their common socioeconomic status correlated positively with a successful placement.

Two studies examine foster parent employment as it relates to foster home satisfaction or success. Gass (1972) examined differences between successful and less successful foster parents. The most successful foster families had fathers who were satisfied with their level of employment. The least successful foster fathers aspired to higher levels of employment. A father's dissatisfaction with his employment is an indicator of potential problems in the foster home. Kraus (1971) looked at the impact of the foster mother's employment. He found that "foster mothers who worked fulltime were as successful as those who did not work, which indicates that the usual reluctance of social agencies to place a child in a foster home when the mother works is unwarranted" (Kraus, 1971:70).

The adult outcomes of foster children have also been examined in relation to location variables (Murphy, 1968). Gilbert (1947) found that if a child was to be placed in a rural area community, support was needed for the placement to be successful. According to Murphy (1968) foster children made the best adjustments in rural and city homes; they experienced the most difficulty in suburban homes. Murphy's earlier study (1964) indicated that foster homes were becoming increasingly suburban. This would indicate that recruitment efforts may be focused in the wrong direction and may further compound placement difficulties. The suburban foster home may provide little continuity in values and culture for the foster child of a low income background.

Kraus (1971), Parker (1966), and Rowe (1976) sought to determine if

age of the foster mother related to foster home success. According to
Kraus (1971), placements were more successful if the foster mother was
46 years old or older. Parker (1966) also found older foster mothers to be
more successful than younger ones. However, Rowe (1976) found the
age of the mother to be unrelated to success at fostering.

Another variable that has been frequently used in foster home success
studies is the number of issue living in the home of the foster parents.
The findings are contradictory. Hunter (1964) and George (1970) found
that the most successful foster parents have no natural children in the
home. Parker (1966) found that childless couples did the best at fostering.
By contrast, Kraus (1971) found placements to be most successful if
foster parents had two children of their own and Wolins (1959) found that
superior foster homes had two or three natural children. Rowe (1976)
found no relationship between successful fostering and the number of
own children.

In a recent study Hunter et al. (1977) sought to determine if satisfaction was related to the length of placement and found "foster parents
could not be differentiated in satisfaction level by whether they had
long-term or short-term placements" (Hunter et al.:8). This study also
compared the satisfaction of foster parents in public and private agencies.
Surprisingly, they found that "no significant differences were found in
overall satisfaction between the foster parents affiliated with a private
agency and those affiliated with the state" (Hunter et al.:13).

Relationship Variables

Several studies look at relationship variables, particularly the relationship that foster parents have with the agency and the child. Aldridge and
Cautley (1975) found that a positive foster mother-social worker relationship in the first six months of foster care increased the mother's satisfaction with her role and enhanced the possibility of success as a foster
parent. Their study indicated that attributes related to foster home satisfaction are formed early in the fostering process. This would reinforce
Kadushin's (1970) belief that there is an increased likelihood for success
if early in the placement process the social worker expresses confidence
in the foster parent. According to Kadushin (1970:230), "expectations are
a powerful force in determining outcome. The self-fulfilling prophecy,
the placebo effect, and the Rosenthal effect all point to this same phenomenon."

Aldridge and Cautley (1975) also found that foster fathers were interested in developing a relationship with workers and desired more frequent contact with workers. "Forty-one percent of the foster fathers indicated interest in seeing the worker more often than they had" (Aldridge and Cautley, 1975:448). This finding is important because the foster father's positive feeling toward worker visitation was found to be a predictor of foster home success. "The length of time spent by the social worker in preparing the foster parents—especially if the foster father was included —had a positive effect on the placement" (Aldridge and Cautley; 1975:6). This same study indicated that foster fathers, more often than foster mothers, provided information regarding difficulties in a child's placement. Foster fathers were removed from significant involvement with workers. Cautley and Aldridge's study would call into question the traditional primary worker involvement with foster mothers and the exclusion of foster fathers.

Cautley and Aldridge (1973), Aldridge and Cautley (1975), and Hampson and Tavormina (1980) all have indicated that foster parents need more contact with the social worker. New foster parents' primary criticism is the unavailability of the worker. Not only new parents but also foster parents that have been in the program for some time need a higher level of turnover. This dissatisfaction is felt particularly in the early stages of placement. Hampson and Tavormina say, "If the placement fails, it may be that the caseworker or local agency is equally at fault with the parents" (Hampson and Tavormina:109). Hunter et al. (1977) found that the setting made a difference regarding one's attitudes toward the social worker. Foster parents in private agencies were basically enthusiastic about worker support but foster parents in public agencies found little support.

As we would expect, the foster parents' relationship with the child affects foster home satisfaction. According to Trasler (1960), both foster parents and child must develop a mutually satisfying relationship for the placement to be stable and secure. However, it appears that the foster mother's relationship with the foster child is a more significant factor than the foster father's relationship to the child. According to Simonds (1973:87), "relationship with the foster mother was the key relationship that determined the success of the placement."

For foster mothers, direct involvement with children in need of care was a major source of gratification (Fanshel, 1966). Fanshel also found that foster mothers caring for infants obtained personal gratifications whereas foster mothers caring for older children obtained social gratifications.

Foster fathers found direct involvement with the children to be less satisfying than did their wives (Fanshel, 1966). Fathers more often chose to be a foster parent and to continue in that role to satisfy their wives or as a form of community service. This lack of enthusiasm for direct paternal involvement is supported in another study by Hunter et al. (1977:11), "Father involvement, as rated by the mother, was not significantly related to overall satisfaction as a foster parent." These studies tend to indicate that the foster father's direct contact with the child is not a major factor related to satisfaction. Cautley and Aldridge's study (1973) came to a different conclusion. They found that the greater the involvement of the foster father with the child, the greater his satisfaction with the role. This study did find that foster fathers were more apt to be involved with foster sons than with foster daughters. And Fanshel (1961) found that foster fathers shared more involvement with older children than with the younger ones. These studies indicate conflicting findings but seem to show that foster fathers prefer to interact with boys rather than with girls and with older rather than younger children.

Personality Variables

Studies examine personality and attitudinal variables as they relate to foster home satisfaction and success. According to Rowe (1976:506), "there is considerable evidence linking foster parents' attitudes with their success at fostering." Other researchers, such as Kinter and Otto (1964), support Krish's contention that there is a relationship between personality adjustment of foster parents and successful fostering.

Rowe (1976), believing that foster parent attitudes affect the quality of care, studied the effect of foster parents' tolerance of differences. This study found that foster parents who could tolerate attitudes and behavior that conflicted with their own value system were more successful as foster parents than those who could not tolerate such attitudes and behavior. Rowe also found that foster parents who held authoritarian attitudes and were extremely devout in their religious beliefs had difficulty in being foster parents.

Eastman (1978) hypothesized that a foster parent's ability to deal with uncertainty would affect foster home satisfaction. However, tolerance of ambiguity did not significantly impact on foster home satisfaction.

Gass (1972) found that couples who scored high on self-disclosure were more successful as foster parents than couples who scored low. For a foster family to be successful, they need to be able to share themselves with the foster child and agency. The successful foster family's high self-disclosure scores apparently affirm this need.

The most successful foster homes tended to have more of a child than a self focus (Kinter and Otto, 1964). The most adequate foster parents gave child-centered rather than self-centered responses.

Murphy's (1968) study indicated that a negative attitude on the part of the foster mother toward the natural parents of the child was detrimental to foster home success. This negativism toward the natural parent is harmful as the natural parent has a viable place in the foster care process which the foster parent should not be allowed to undermine.

Fanshel (1966) noted that foster mothers caring for infants have the most difficulty with separation while those mothers caring for older children have the least difficulty. He also found, but Hunter et al. did not, that the foster mothers of infants have the highest level of satisfaction.

What has really been learned about foster home success and satisfaction from these various studies? Among studies that examine demographic variables, Delgado's (1978) study seems highly promising in terms of potential use to the practitioner. His study emphasizes the importance of foster parent and foster child sharing a similar socioeconomic background. This has implications for matching child with a foster family. Kraus' (1971) indicated that foster mothers who worked were as successful at fostering as those who chose not to work. And Murphy's (1968) study on foster home location indicates that recruitment efforts might be better channeled to the rural and city areas rather than suburbia. Relationship variables were found to be important—the relationships of both foster mother and father to the agency and child seems to make a difference as to the level of satisfaction although the findings are conflicting. Among personality variables, foster parents who are capable of tolerating differences, have the ability to disclose themselves, and are child-focused appear to be quite successful at fostering. Foster parents who hold authoritarian attitudes, are extremely devout in their religious faith, and are hostile toward the child's natural parents seem to fare less well in fostering.

Legal Issues

Court litigation has broadened the scope of foster parent rights. One of the crucial concerns in the legal realm is determining the residual rights of the natural parents, the rights of the foster child and foster parents. "All of these relationships take place within a legal frame of reference although many of the more subtle legal questions remain ill defined and untested" (Lawder et al., 1974:13). Hampson and Tavormina (1980) recently stated that foster parents had no legal or parental rights. This is an overstatement. Foster parents do have some rights—rights largely won due to court litigation. Their rights remain secondary to those of the natural parents and agency. As long as the casework goal for a child is reunification with his natural family the natural parents will hold rights above those of foster parents. Only with a child freed for adoption can the foster parents hope to have a say.

The California Court of Appeals did rule that should a foster child not be able to return to his own home the persons with whom the child had been living (namely the foster parents) would be given first consideration in custody decisions (Katz, 1976). This ruling supports the concept of psychological parenting as espoused by Goldstein et al. (1973). Also, the child's needs for continuity of relationship has emerged as a critical variable in decision-making" (Wiltse, 1979:11).

The California Court of Appeals' ruling challenged many pre-existing policies of agencies throughout this country. In the past, agencies have been extremely reluctant to allow foster parent adoption. Only if a child was considered otherwise unadoptable would foster parents even be considered as adoptive parents. This court ruling has caused many agencies to change longstanding policies that forbade foster parent adoption.

Another right foster parents gained through court action was the right to participate in a pre-removal hearing if a child has been in their home for longer than one year. The United States District Court ruled in the Organization of Foster Families vs. Dumpson that foster parents do have the right to be heard in a pre-removal hearing. The court made this ruling on the grounds that the pre-removal hearing actually was a right of the foster child since his future was at stake (Katz, 1976). The pre-removal hearing serves to protect both the foster child and foster parent against the agency's almost absolute power regarding placement moves (Albert, 1978).

Foster parents have also wanted a voice in custody proceedings. In the mid-1970s many agencies began permanency planning for children in their care. These plans were subject to review—either administratively, judicially, or by citizen group. Whatever the format foster parents want to be involved in the decisions that impact on the lives of foster children in their care and subsequently impact on their own lives. At the present time, there has been no concerted effort to incorporate foster parents into permanency planning unless they are approached regarding adoption, quasi-adoption, subsidized adoption, or guardianship of a child who has been in their home for a number of years.

One other legal issue needs to be addressed. In the 1970s some state associations and private agencies began to encourage foster parents to obtain liability insurance. This insurance would protect foster parents against a damage suit should a foster child in their care be injured and would cover damages a foster child might incur while in their care (New Jersey Home Developers' Manual, 1976; Georgia Foster Parent Manual, 1978). This trend toward foster parent liability insurance coverage should continue.

Prognosis

Change has occurred in the foster care system and will continue to occur.

Agencies need to constantly reexamine their policies. Historically, agencies have resisted change and most foster parent rights have been won through the courts. Foster parent adoption and pre-removal hearings were not routinely employed before the court decisions ruled favorably on these issues. When foster parents cannot effectively be heard by the agency, they will continue to seek solutions through the court system.

The status of foster parents needs to be upgraded. Foster parenthood must become more attractive. Foster parenting must be viewed as an important task—one where individuals are making a significant contribution to society by parenting other people's children. This task is made more difficult in the social climate of the 1980s where women find childrearing less attractive than they have in the past. Increasing pay and status of foster parents may add professionalism to the role and would help make fostering a desirable alternative to out-of-home employment.

Foster parent associations have helped to improve foster homes throughout this country. They have provided foster parents a collective voice and increased power as well as educational opportunities. Foster parent training developed largely through federal grant money and the support of the National Foster Parents' Association. Progress has been made to the extent that many states now mandate training.

In the 1980s there will be an increased need to prevent children from entering foster care. Parental responsibility must not be easily abdicated. More support services will be needed for families. And should a child enter foster care there must be increased use of contracts, permanency planning, and formal review, either judicially, administratively, or through a citizens review board.

Foster care systems must also become more efficient. Accountability and evaluation were keywords of the 1970s—they will continue to be important in the 1980s. The high cost of fostering necessitates efficiency and a search for better alternatives.

Finally, the relationship between theory, research, and practice needs to be examined and developed. At this point in time theory is sorely lacking. Almost none of the research is tied to a theoretical base. However, research has built an expanded body of knowledge that is useful to the social work practitioner. This knowledge needs to be translated into the practitioner's language and made readily available to him. Research findings and implications need to be succinct and clearly stated. We have now reached the stage where we need to apply what we know as well as to continue to expand the body of knowledge.

REFERENCES

Alaska Health and Social Services Manual, Juneau: Division of Social Services, Department of Health and Social Services, 1978.

Albert, Marilyn, "Pre-removal appeal procedure in foster family care: A Connecticut example." *Child Welfare* 57(5):285-297, 1978.

Aldridge, Martha J., and Patricia W. Cautley, "The importance of worker availability in the functioning of new foster homes." *Child Welfare* 54(6):444-453, 1975.

——— "Placing siblings in the same foster home." *Child Welfare* 55(2):85-93, 1976.

Anderson, Sheila, "Foster parent organizations: How a provincewide federation was formed in British Columbia." Pp. 68-72 in *On Fostering.* New York: Child Welfare League of America, Inc., 1973.

Arizona Family Foster Home Licensing Standards, Phoenix: Arizona, Department of Economic Security, 1977.

Atherton, Charles R., "Acting decisively in foster care." *Social Work* 19(6): 658,741, 1974.

Babcock, Charlotte, "Some psychodynamic factors in foster parenthood - Part I." *Child Welfare* 44(9):485-493, 1965.

Barnhill, Laurence R., "Healthy family systems." *The Family Coordinator* 28(1):94-100, 1979.

Boyd, Lawrence H., Jr., and Linda L. Remy, "Is foster parent training worthwhile?" *Social Service Review* 52(2);275-296, 1978.

Bryce, Marvin E., and Roger C. Ehlert, "144 foster children." *Child Welfare* 50(9):499-503, 1971.

Calhoun, John, "The 1980 Child Welfare Act: A Turning Point for Children and Troubled Families." *Children Today* 9(5): 2-4, 1980.

Cautley, Patricia W., and Martha J. Aldridge, "Becoming a foster parent: Summary of a study of new foster parents and their experiences." Madison: Wisconsin Department of Health and Social Services, 1973.

―――― "Predicting success for new foster parents." *Social Work* 20(1):48-53, 1975.

Claburn, W., S. Magura, and W. Resnick, "Periodic review of foster care: A brief national assessment." *Child Welfare* 55(6): 395-405, 1976.

Clement, Priscilla Ferguson, "Families and foster care: Philadelphia in the late nineteenth century." *Social Service Review* 53(3): 406-420, 1979.

Coyne, Ann, "Techniques for recruiting foster homes for mentally retarded children." *Child Welfare* 57(2): 123-131, 1978.

Daniels, Robert, and John A. Brown, "Foster parents and the agency." *Children Today* 2(3): 25-27, 1973.

Davies, Linda J., and David C. Bland, "The use of foster parents as role models for parents." *Child Welfare* 57(4): 381-386, 1978.

Delgado, Melvin, "A Hispanic foster parent program." *Child Welfare* 57(7): 427-431, 1978.

Dinnage, Rosemary, and M. L. Kellmer Pringle, Foster home care: Facts and fallacies. London: Longmans, Green, and Co., 1967.

Drydyk, Joan, Bea Menderville, and Laura Bender, "Foster parenting a retarded child: The Arizona story." *Children Today* 9 (July-August):10 + , 1980.

Eastman, Kathleen S., Tolerance of ambiguity as a component of foster home satisfaction. Doctoral dissertation. Iowa State University, 1978.

―――― "The foster family in a systems theory perspective." *Child Welfare* 58(9): 564-570, 1979.

Ellis, Lillian, "Sharing parents with strangers: The role of the group home foster family's own children." Pp. 92-97 in *On fostering*. New York: Child Welfare League of America, Inc., 1973.

Fanshel, David, Toward more understanding of foster parents. Doctoral dissertation. Columbia University, 1960.

―――― "Specialization within the foster parent role - Part I: Differences between the foster parents of infants and foster parents of older children." *Child Welfare* 40(3): 17-21, 1961.

―――― *Foster parenthood: A role analysis*. Minneapolis: University of Minnesota Press, 1966.

―――― "The role of foster parents in the future of foster care." Pp. 228-240 in H. D. Stone (Ed.), *Foster care in question: A national reassessment by twenty-one experts*. New York: Child Welfare League of America, Inc., 1970.

―――― "The exit of children from foster care: An interim research report." *Child Welfare* 50(2):65-81, 1971.

Fanshel, David, and Eugene B. Shinn, *Children in foster care: A longitudinal investigation*. New York: Columbia University Press, 1978.

Felker, Evelyn H., "Why are foster parents so hung up on values?" *Child Welfare* 57(4):259-261, 1978.

Festinger, Trudy Bradley, "The New York court review of children in foster care." *Child Welfare* 54(4): 211-245, 1975.

Finkelstein, Nadia Erlich, "Children in limbo." *Social Work* 25(March 1980): 100-105.

Freeman, Henry, "Foster home care for mentally retarded children: Can it work?" *Child Welfare* 57(2):113-121, 1978.

Freund, Virginia W., "Evaluation of a self-approval method for inducting foster parents." *Smith College Studies in Social Work* 46(2):114-126, 1976.

Gabrovic, Audrey, "Participation of active foster parents in the study of new applicants." Pp. 19-23 in *On fostering*. New York: Child Welfare League of America, Inc., 1973.

Galaway, Burt, "Clarifying the role of foster parents." *Children Today* 1(4):32-33, 1972.

Garber, Michael, Sister Mary Patrick, and Lourdes Casal, "The ghetto as a source of foster homes." *Child Welfare* 49(May 1970):246-251.

Garrett, Beatrice L., "The rights of foster parents." *Children* 17(3):113, 1970.

Gass, Mary Pat, Foster parents: An attempt to describe foster parents with respect to their adequacy and to discriminate between foster and non-foster parents. Doctoral dissertation. Purdue University, 1972.

George, Victor, *Foster care: Theory and practice*. London: Routledge and K. Paul, 1970.

Georgia Foster Parent Manual, Atlanta: Georgia Department of Human Resources, Division of Family and Children Services, 1978.

Gilbert, Louise, "Foster home care in rural areas." *Journal of Social Casework* 28(2): 67-72, 1947.

Glassberg, Eunice, "Are foster homes hard to find?" *Child Welfare* 44(8): 453-460, 1965.

Goldstein, Harriet, "What's Jewish about Jewish child care?" *Journal of Jewish Communal Service* 49(4): 131-136, 1973.

Goldstein, Joseph, Anna Freud, and Albert J. Solnit, *Beyond the best interests of the child*. New York: The Free Press, 1973.

Gordon, James S., "Alternative group foster homes: A new place for young people to live." *Psychiatry* 39 (November 1976): 339-354.

Gross, Barbara Danzger, Bernard J. Shuman, and D. Tracey Magid, *Using the one-way mirror to train foster parents in child development,"* *Child Welfare* 57(10):685-688, 1978.

Guerney, Louise F., *Foster parent training: A manual for parents*. University Park: Pennsylvania State University, 1975.

Hampson, Robert B., and Joseph B. Tavormina, "Feedback from the experts: A study of foster mothers." *Social Work* 25 (March 1980):108-112.

Harling, Paul R., and Joan K. Haines, "Specialized foster homes for severely mistreated children." *Children Today* 9(July-August 1980):16-18.

Hikel, Virginia, "Fostering the troubled child." Pp. 24-28 in *On fostering*. New York: Child Welfare League of America, Inc., 1973.

Hunter L., "Fosterhomes for teenagers." *Children* 11(6):234 + , 1964.

Hunter, Liz, Linda Kelsey, and Patti McCabe, The unsung art of fostering. Master's thesis. University of Connecticut at Storrs, 1977.

Jenkins, Shirley, "Duration of foster care: Some relevant antecedent variables." *Child Welfare* 46(8): 450-455, 1967.

Jones, Evan O., "A study of those who cease to foster." *British Journal of Social Work* 5(1): 31-41, 1975.

Jones, Martha L., "Stopping foster care drift: A review of legislation and special programs." *Child Welfare* 57(9): 571-580, 1978.

Jones, Martha L., and John L. Biesecker, "Training in permanency planning: Using what is known." *Child Welfare* 59(8): 481-489, 1980.

Kadushin, Alfred, *Adopting older children*. New York: Columbia University Press, 1970.

——— "Child welfare strategy in the coming years: An overview." Pp. 1-50 in *Child welfare strategy in the coming years*. United States Department of Health, Education, and Welfare, Office of Human Development Services, Administration for Children, Youth, and Families, 1978,.

Katz, Sanford N., "The changing legal status of foster parents." *Children Today* 5(6): 11-13, 1976

Kay, Neil, "Foster parents as resources." Pp. 69-77 in R. Tod(Ed.), *Social work in foster care*. London: Longman Group Ltd. (a), 1971.

——— "A systematic approach to selecting foster parents." Pp. 39-50 in R. Tod (Ed.), *Social work in foster care*. London: Longman Group Ltd. (b), 1971.

Kennedy, Ruby, "A foster parent looks at foster care." Pp. 51-59 in *On fostering*. New York: Child Welfare League of America, Inc., 1973.

Kent, Marilyn O., "Remarriage: A family systems perspective." *Social Casework* 25 (March 1980): 146-153.

Kentucky Community Services Manual to Families and Children, Frankford: Department for Human Resources, Bureau for Social Services, 1978.

Kinter, R., and H. A. Otto, "The family-strength concept and foster family selection." *Child Welfare* 43(7):359-364, 1964.

Kline, Draza, and Helen Mary Overstreet, *Foster care of children: nurture and treatment*. New York: Columbia University Press, 1972.

Knox, David, "Trends in marriage and the family—the 1980s." *Family Relations* 29 (2):145-150, 1980.

Kraus, Jonathan, "Predicting success of foster placements for school-age children." *Social Work* 16(1):63-72, 1971.

Lawder, Elizabeth A., "Toward a more scientific understanding of foster family care." *Child Welfare* 43(2): 57-63, 1964.

Lawder, E., R. Andrews, and J. Parsons, *Five models of foster family group homes*. New York: Child Welfare League of America, Inc., 1974.

Levine, A., "Substitute child care: Recent research and its implications." *Welfare in Review* 10(1): 1-7, 1972.

Lindberg, Dwaine R., and Anne W. Wosmek, "The use of family sessions in foster home care." *Social Casework* 44(3): 137-141, 1963.

Maas, Henry S., "Children in long-term foster care." *Child Welfare* 48(6): 321-333, 1969.

Macintyre, J. McEwan, "Adolescence, identity, and foster family care." *Children* 17 (November 1970): 213-218.

Mandell, B., *Where are the children: A class analysis of foster care and adoption*. Lexington, Mass.: Lexington Books, 1973.

Massachusetts Social Services Policy Manual, Boston: The Commonwealth of Massachusetts Department of Public Welfare, 1978.

McCoy, Jacqueline, "The motives and conflicts of foster parenthood." *Children* 9(6): 222-226, 1962.

Meyer, Margrit, "Family ties and the institutional child." *Children* 16(6): 226-231, 1969.

Mississippi Rules and Regulations for Maintaining Minimum Standards of Foster Family Homes for Children, Jackson: Division of Social Services, Mississippi Department of Public Welfare, 1979.

Monane, Joseph H., *A sociology of human systems*. New York: Meredith Publishing Co., 1967.

Moore, Pauline, "Foster family care for visually impaired children." *Children Today* 5(4): 11-15, 1976.

Murphy, H.B.M. "Foster home variables and adult outcomes." *Mental Hygiene* 48(4): 587-599, 1964.

——— "Predicting duration of foster care." *Child Welfare* 47(2):76-84, 1968.

Naughton, Francis X., "Foster home placement as an adjunct to residential treatment." *Social Casework* 38(6):288-295, 1957.

Nebraska's Guide for Foster Parents, Lincoln: Division of Social Services, Nebraska Department of Public Welfare, 1978.

Nevada Standards for Foster Home Care of Children, Carson City: Welfare Division, State of Nevada Department of Human Resources, 1977.

New Jersey Foster Home Developers Manual, Trenton: Division of Youth and Family Services, Department of Institutions and Agencies.

Pare, A., and J. Torczyner, "The interests of children and the interests of the state:

Rethinking the conflict between child welfare policy and foster care practice." *Journal of Sociology and Social Work* 4(8): 1224-1244, 1977.

Parker, R., *Decision in child care*. London: George Allen and Unwin, 1966.

Pedosuk, Leona, and Elizabeth Ratcliffe, "Using foster parent to help foster parents: A Canadian experiment." *Child Welfare* 58(7): 467-470, 1979.

Penn, John V., "A model for training foster parents in behavior modification techniques." *Child Welfare* 57(3): 175-180, 1978.

Poertner, John, and Charles A. Rapp, "Information system design in foster care." *Social Work* 25 (March 1980): 114-119.

Radinsky, Elizabeth, "Provisions for care: Foster family care." Pp. 52-81 in H. D. Stone (Ed.), *Foster care in question: A national reassessment by twenty-one experts.* New York: Child Welfare League of America, Inc., 1970.

Reistroffer, Mary, "A university extension course for foster parents." *Children* 15(1): 11-15, 1968.

"Participation of foster parents in decision-making: The concept of collegiality." *Child Welfare* 51(1): 25-29, 1972.

Rose, J., "Re-evaluation of the concept of separation for child welfare." *Child Welfare* 41(10): 444-458, 1962.

Rosendorf, Shirley, "Joining together to help foster children: Foster parents form a national association." *Children Today* 1(1): 26, 1972.

Rothschild, Ann M., "An agency evaluates its foster home services." *Child Welfare* 53(1):42-50, 1974.

Rowe, David C., "Attitudes, social class, and the quality of foster care." *Social Service Review* 50(3): 506-514, 1976.

Russell, Thomas H., and Jayne M. Silberman, "Improving the delivery of specialized foster care systems." *Social Casework* 24(July 1979): 402-407.

Sacks, Gerda G., and Ruth Case, "Foster home recruitment - problems and solutions in the large and small communities." *Journal of Jewish Communal Service* 44 (4): 350-359, 1968.

Schott, Max, Jr., "Iowa assesses its foster care program." *The Social and Rehabilitation Record* 1(10): 9-11, 1974.

Simonds, John P., "A foster home for crisis placements." *Child Welfare* 52(2): 82-90, 1973.

Stanley, Ruth Light, "The group method in foster home studies." In Robert Tod (Ed.), *Social work in foster care*. London: Longman Group Ltd., 1971.

Stein, Theodore J., Eileen D. Gambrill, and Kermit T. Wiltse, "Contracts and outcome in foster care." *Social Work* 22(2): 148-149, 1977.

Stone, Helen D., "Foster parenting a retarded child: The new curriculum?" *Children Today* 9 (July-August): 11 + , 1980.

———— *Leaders' guide: foster parenting an adolescent*. New York: Child Welfare League of America, Inc., 1978.

Torczyner, J., and Arleen Pare, "The influence of environmental factors in foster care." *Social Service Review* 53 (September 1979): 358-377.

Trasler, G., *In place of parents*. London: Routledge and K. Paul, 1960.

Wilkes, J. R., "The impact of fostering on the foster family." *Child Welfare* 53(6): 373-379, 1974.

Wiltse, Kermit T., "Current issues and new trends in foster care." Pp. 51-89 in *Child Welfare strategy in the coming years*. United States Department of Health, Education, and Welfare, Office of Human Development Services, Administration for Children, Youth, and Families, 1978.

———— "Foster Care in the 1970's: A Decade of Change." *Children Today* 8(3): 10-14, 1979.

Wolins, Martin, Selection of foster parents: Early stages in the development of a screen. Doctoral dissertation. Columbia University, 1959.

Wyoming Social Services Manual, Cheyenne: Wyoming Department of Health and Social Services, 1979.

ANALYTICAL ESSAY

Kris Jeter

Research project directors are eliminating the word "social" from their study titles and stated intentions. Investigators are cleansing their work of intervention strategies and behavior change requirements in order to retain meagre government funding or to garner new support from the overflooded foundation arena. It is the trend once again in our society to kill the messenger, rather than the sender of the message. Funding is divested from researchers who are suspected of altering and tampering with human kind. Or are these investigators simply aware of the subtle movements in society and observing, recording, and reporting these changes in a systematic order? It is a time of uncertainty for researchers who study the changing roles of women and men living in alternative family forms.

What is the effect of research on societal change? How are we to conceptualize and communicate professionally about our research and therapy with families, especially with those who live in alternative forms? How are we to apply research findings to members of alternative form families with whom we work? This analytical essay searches for answers to these three questions and shares thoughts ignited by Margrit Eichler in her newly published book, *The Double Standard,* and by David Gordon, in his recently printed book, *Therapeutic Metaphors*. These books examine how we think and perceive the lives of women and men and families of any form.

Research is a careful, systematic investigation to discover new trends and facts with safeguards determined and announced regarding all possible consequences of the study process. Research is searching for new knowledge using a scientific method with rational and logical thinking. Each society has a status quo with its own body of knowledge which the powerless seek to use to obtain their power. Power holders strive to control knowledge because knowledge is power; research for the powerless is a slow process. The effect of new knowledge depends on its actualization and acceptance in society. Generally with time the new

Dr. Jeter is a Trainer and principal at Beacon Associates, Ltd., Inc., Newark, DE.

121

becomes the old. Eichler points out that research is the search for significant differences leading us to forget and diminish the similarities. The researcher in proving the existence and viability of alternate family forms may continue unintentionally to reinforce the traditional family form by emphasizing the importance of the traditional family.

How are we to conceptualize research about human behavior and alternative family forms? Alternative family forms can irritate the empowered because roles may be assumed in these families by atypical people. For instance, in a commuter marriage, a woman may be a traveling wage earner and a man may be caring for children as a homemaker or as a worker in a dual career family. Eichler speaks specifically to culturally determined gender roles and biologically determined sex roles which have become merged together due to the difficulty in distinguishing differences between them.

How are we to conceptualize and communicate about research on alternative family forms to prevent a political backlash? Eichler discusses specific recommendations for persons creating a human behavior science studying both females and males singularly, in families, and in society.

1. We must consistently de-masculinize our language to assist us to perceive in our esconced thought patterns the exclusion of women.
2. Femininity and masculinity are the consequence of social factors and are constantly changing and should be limited in use to "empirically established configurations of variables which are differentiated by sex." Likewise, the use of masculinity-femininity scales rigidifies sex roles stereotypes.
3. The reporting of sex differences alone distorts reality. A finding of "no sex difference" is significant and contributes to the gestalt of the research.
4. Words which denote quality of action such as emotionality and rationality are to be regarded as individual continua that vary independently and which may describe the same action.
5. The family is not simply a functional unit, rather it is "a complex pattern of relationships between different role incumbents."
6. Work is to be classified as socially necessary or less necessary rather than paid and unpaid.
7. Sex role socialization does not incorporate a positive sense of sex into a healthy self image.
8. The current definition of social classes and their measurement excludes women and must be reconceptualized and restructured.

How are we to apply research findings to members of alternative form families with whom we work? What can therapists do to teach their clients from alternative family forms how to deal with possible feelings of isolation, prejudice, and definsiveness they might experience? David Gordon provides a valuable instruction on the formation of therapeutic metaphors that translate the world of everyday behaviors and interactions into the language of the people. His book, *Therapeutic Metaphors* need not be reading limited to clinicians. It is important reading for communicators, educators, and researchers. Professionals can employee metaphors to deepen the level of communication, feelings, and understanding.

The word metaphor, is derived from the Greek words, "meta," meaning over, and "pherein," meaning to carry. Metaphors as verbal representations of experiences carry us over personal and communication hurdles. Metaphors in the form of anecdotes, epic poems, fables, fairy tales, gossip, idioms, jokes, movies, novels, parables, poetry, songs, and stories have through the world's history transmitted from one generation to the next the cultural, historical, moral, and problem solving codes. Metaphors contain problem solving experiences.

Our brain contains personal experiences and experiences of ages past. It is the model of the world and when we realize that each person's brain model of the world is different, communication can be intensified. We are then able to meet the other person at their model of the world.

A trans derivational search is the process of reviewing our models of the world to understand our present experience. When communicating and wishing to use an applicable metaphor, the first step is to image in the entire situation, identifying realistic goals, the problem, the usual course of events which tends to be repetitive in other situations, the desired outcome, and the cast of significant persons and their interrelationships. After obtaining this information a story line is constructed. Any setting which provides equivalent characters, character relationships, and events will be suitable for the metaphor. Nouns and verbs should be vague so that the most appropriate meaning can be supplied by the listener. Feelings are nominalized, for instance, "I'm angry" becomes "anger" so that the listener can look at the feeling objectively and amplify the sensation suitable to the situation. Specific names and suggested commands can be imbedded into the metaphor to assist in behavior change.

We each have one sense that is more highly developed than the other four and use this sense—either auditory, kinesthetic, olfactory, visual, or taste—the most. Our speech tends to indicate this most trusted sense in the form of sensory-specific predicates. We also use different senses and sensory-specific predicates to describe different experiences. To facilitate a change in behavior, one uses the senses and accompanying predicate for support. To open communication between two individuals who speak in different sensory-specific predicates, ask them to share one sensory system.

Metaphorical communication can be used to assist people to view problems and issues in a holistic fashion and to contemplate new solutions. Metaphors can be used to break the double standard by focusing on similarities of humans and families. For instance, when communicating about the viability of alternate family forms, we could create a metaphor to broaden the definition of a family to include traditional and alternative family forms. The double standard for judging families could be examined and "a family is a family is a family" could result. The metaphor would be constructed to awaken all of the senses with the use of action verbs and to stimulate personal involvement with open ended phases.

SELECTIVE GUIDE TO CURRENT REFERENCE SOURCES ON ALTERNATIVE FAMILY FORMS AND LIFE STYLES

Jonathan B. Jeffery

This section of *Marriage and Family Review* is the third in a series of reference sources pertaining to the theme of each issue. The sources listed here will provide additional information on the topic of variant family forms and life-styles. This information is selective, not comprehensive, and the material will generally be current.

The usefulness of the source is often indicated by sample keyword suggestions, however, the reader should consider other possible subject terms and all synonymous words when searching these sources.

Assistance of a librarian may be required to utilize computer data bases or to respond to individual research interests.

1a. *Indexing and Abstracting Sources. Publisher, start date, and frequency of publication are noted.*

Education Index. New York, Wilson, 1929-   , monthly.
>   See: Married Women-Employment, Mothers-Employment, One-Parent Family, Collective Settlements.

Inventory of Marriage and Family Literature. Minneapolis, MI, Minnesota Family Study Center and the Institute of Life Insurance, 1967-   .
>   See: Dual Career Family, Cohabitation, Childlessness, Single-Parent.

New York Times Index. New York, Times, 1851-   , semimonthly.
>   See: Marriages

Psychological Abstracts. Lancaster, PA, American Psychological Association, 1927-   , monthly.

Mr. Jeffery is Associate Librarian, Reference Department, University of Delaware, Newark, DE 19711.

See: Cohabitation, Marital Relations, Family Relations, Communes, Kibbutz Single Parents, Marital Status, Occupational Choice.

Readers' Guide to Periodical Literature. New York, Wilson, 1905- , semimonthly.

See: Marriage, Family, Unmarried Couples, Single People.

Sage Family Studies Abstracts. Beverly Hills, Sage Publications, 1979- , published 4 times a year.

See: Cohabitation, Dual-Career Family, Childless Couples, Single Parent, Communal Living.

Social Sciences Citation Index. Philadelphia, Institute for Scientific Information, 1969- , published 3 times a year.

See: Keywords in titles.

See: Citation Index.

Social Sciences Index. New York, Wilson, 1974- , quarterly.

See: Cohabitation, Single Parent Family.

Sociological Abstracts. New York, Sociological Abstracts, 1952- , published 6 times a year.

See: Marriage.

Women Studies Abstracts. New York, Rush, 1972- , quarterly.

See: Single Parents, Dual Careers, Cohabitation, Childlessness, Family Structure.

1b. *On-Line Bibliographic Data Bases. Examples of search entry points are given for selected data bases. Consult a librarian for search formulation.*

ERIC-Educational Resources Information Clearinghouse (includes *Resources in Education* and *Current Index to Journals in Education*).

Use: keywords.

Use: *Thesaurus of ERIC Descriptors.*

MAGAZINE INDEX-scans popular magazines (includes coverage in *Readers' Guide to Periodical Literature*).

Use: keywords.

NATIONAL NEWSPAPER INDEX-(includes *Christian Science Monitor, New York Times,* and *Wall Street Journal*).

Use: keywords.

POPULATION BIBLIOGRAPHY

Use: keywords.

Use: *Population/Family Planning Thesaurus.*

PSYCHINFO-(includes *Psychological Abstracts*).
  Use: keywords.
  Use: *Thesaurus of Psychological Index Terms,*
SOCIAL SCISEARCH-(corresponds to printed *Social Science Citation Index*)
  Use: keywords from titles.
  Use: citation to existing literature.
SOCIOLOGICAL ABSTRACTS
  Use: keywords.

2. *Journal Listings and Selected Journal Titles*

Ulrichs International Periodicals Directory, 20th ed., 1981, New York, R.R. Bowker Co, annual.
  See: Sociology, and Psychology in subject index. Selected journal titles: *Communities: a Journal of Cooperative Living, Family Coordinator, Journal of Comparative Family Studies, Journal of Marriage and the Family, Journal of Sex Research. Marriage and Family Review, Journal of Family Issues.*

3. *Books*

Cumulative Book Index, New York, Wilson, 1933- , monthly.
  See: Family-United States, Single People, Unmarried Couples.

4. *Handbooks*

Akey, DS, ed. *Encyclopedia of Associations,* 16th ed, Detroit, Gale Research Co., 1981, 3 vols.
  See: keyword subject index under marriage and family terms.
  See: possible relevant associations include Center for the Study of Democratic Institutions, Institute on the Family and the Bureaucratic Society, and Synergy Power Institute.

5. *U.S. Government Publications*

"Census of Population," *Subject Bibliography* 181, Washington, D.C., Government Printing Office, 1978, 30p.

Statistical Abstract of the United States. Washington, D.C., Government Printing Office, 1980, annual.
> See: Marriage statistics, (eg. statistics on unmarried couples, percent single).

6. *Audiovisual Programs*

Nordquist, Joan, *Audiovisuals for Women*, Jefferson, N.C., McFarland, 1980.
> See: Examples of entries include *Communal Living-an Alternative*, under videotapes section, and *Open Marriage*, under recordings section.

7. *Proceedings of Meetings*

Interdok, Directory of Published Proceedings, Harrison, N.Y., Interdok Corporation, monthly.
> See: indexing by keywords in the name of the conference, the sponsors, and the title.

8. *Guides to Upcoming Meetings*

World Meetings: Social & Behavioral Sciences, Human Services & Management. New York, N.Y., MacMillan Publishing Co., quarterly.
> See: keyword subject index, sponsor directory.